A Career in Banking

Sheila Black
and John Brennan

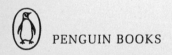

PENGUIN BOOKS

PENGUIN BOOKS

Published by the Penguin Group
27 Wrights Lane, London W8 5TZ, England
Viking Penguin Inc., 40 West 23rd Street, New York, New York 10010, USA
Penguin Books Australia Ltd, Ringwood, Victoria, Australia
Penguin Books Canada Ltd, 2801 John Street, Markham, Ontario, Canada L3R 1B4
Penguin Books (NZ) Ltd, 182–190 Wairau Road, Auckland 10, New Zealand

Penguin Books Ltd, Registered Offices: Harmondsworth, Middlesex, England

First published 1988

Filmset in Linotron 202 Melior

Typeset, printed and bound in Great Britain by
Hazell Watson & Viney Limited
Member of BPCC plc
Aylesbury Bucks

To our own bank managers
past and present,
but only the ones we have liked

Contents

Introduction

Every morning 380,000 people in Britain head for work in banks. Small groups of chatting counter clerks gather outside their high street branches waiting for an under-manager to arrive with the keys. From commuter estates across the nation managers leave for work in their graded company cars. At City of London railway stations the trains disgorge hordes of men and women, who make for the skyscraper towers and the baronial-hall headquarters buildings of the banks, where chauffeur-clean cars are delivering soberly tailored senior excutives.

Long before the doors open for business at more than 14,500 branches, permanently frowning young men and women have been scanning their dealing screens within the banks and making the first of the day's innumerable telephone calls to all over the world, to wherever there is money and money dealings. These are the foreign exchange dealers, the currency brokers whose work is geared to the unsocial hours of international trading, a frantic market that rarely slows down as deals follow the sun through satellite links around the globe.

Merchant bankers arrive to a day's diary filled with deceptively informal meetings, where the customers are corporations and the conversations start in millions of pounds.

From the £4,000-a-year clerk to the £250,000-a-year chief executive, today's bankers range across the spectrum of talent and ambition. School-leavers and graduates, careerists and clock-watchers rub shoulders in halls dedicated mainly to using or lending other people's money.

None of the standard cartoon images quite fit. The pin-stripe-suited bank manager sternly advising rogue customers to 'stay within their limits' still finds an echo in some branches. But today's manager might equally be touring local firms to drum up business.

He might be soft-selling one of his group's other services, advising on investments, tax problems, home loans or business development loans. 'He' may be a 'she', and either or both could be working far from any local high street branch.

The branches are still the front line of the business, though some modern bankers might have only the most fleeting experience of the counter trade.

Supporting those branches are the 'back-room' departments, the hidden reaches of an industry that employs computer staff, specialists in corporate or personal tax, people who may never even see a customer. These departments, some of which may be bigger than any single branch, cope with the specialized elements – foreign trade, hire purchase, insurance, marketing, property management and handling close on 300 million credit card transactions every year.

Few people are aware of these vast support services unless they are devotees of the financial journals or City pages. Merchant banks hit the headlines in connection with takeover bids or the privatization of nationalized industries, or, quite often these days, as launchers of private companies on to the public stock market.

Many career guides ignore all but the high street bankers and, perhaps, the Bank of England (which is, incidentally, every bit as approachable as the others). We feel that, because competition for bank jobs has become so fierce these days, the job-hunter must be aware of all possible career targets and be backed by all the know-how and other ammunition he can acquire to help him to score – first with an interview and then with the job itself.

Therefore, besides being practical about pay, hours, conditions, training and the rest, we have tried to give a picture of what banking is, even down to the public perception of bankers themselves. Along with the history, the background, the story of how and why banks were born, we have given a glimpse of the future.

You may well wonder if you need to know all this.

We think you do. These days employers are looking for bright young people, people with interest, enthusiasm and, above all, with understanding. We believe that the best applicant and the best interviewee will be the one who knows what banking was, is and may be.

Any job-hunter who has researched his subject has a good chance of being successful. He can relax at the interview as if he has studied well for an exam. He will know that he knows as much as, if not more than, his interviewer. He can be self-confident, calm, relaxed.

Why leave it to luck when professionalism probably works better? Learn your subject.

There's another point. Proper research will help you to clarify your own thoughts, hopes and ambitions. You will know for sure whether banking is really for you.

A banking career has many advantages – fringe benefits such as cheap loans and mortgages and an annual bonus are only some of them. Being part of a fast-changing world, full of opportunity, is another.

Don't get the idea that all bankers conform to the traditional carefully groomed image. Banking is a profoundly stable business, but it is also a business in the process of change.

Good luck.

1 Working in a Bank

1 Who Does What?

Most bankers work in the country's 14,500 branches. There are around 300,000 of these high street staff, and a further 70–80,000 in the many other jobs at head offices, in specialist departments, and in merchant and international banks. With few exceptions, most of those bankers started in one of the clerical grades 1 to 4.

Grade 1

If you start your banking career in a branch, the early days will be devoted to showing you round and explaining the jobs you will be doing in the first few months. New staff are also given a programmed learning book which spells out in detail the precise procedures for each of the jobs of the branch.

From the start it is likely that you will be asked to help sort out the day's incoming mail and to list incoming cheques on a machine. Grade 1 staff may have to cope with preparing statements and helping to sort out arrangements for customers to receive them. There is always filing to do and an endless round of jobs which help to keep the clerical work of your branch running efficiently.

Once you get really used to the work you will be answering the telephone and dealing with customers' queries, although no one expects a new staff member to be able to deal with complex requests. You will be expected to pass on any questions or callers that present problems you cannot solve. You may meet customers who come in for a look at their statements, but you will not at this stage be doing the counter cashier's work.

It is all very much routine, and often a chore, but it should be interesting if it is new to you. If you're in a local branch in the area where you live, you will be interested to recognize local celebrities, or people whom you have read about in the local paper. You will get to know certain customers – the shopkeeper who comes in daily with the takings, or the small businessman who comes in less often.

You may get a title, for example remittance clerk. At one time you would have been laboriously adding and subtracting seemingly innumerable cheques; these days you will list them on to machines, code them to allow the computers to read and sort them according to each bank code number, and hope that the totals agree before you prepare them for sending off to the clearing department.

You may become a terminal operator. All branches are linked to a computer network, and your job will be to feed information through to the terminal so that customers' accounts and statements can be kept up to date. You also get feedback from the computer, such as customer account balances, and you will have that data on the screens in your branch.

Learning how to use a computer terminal has become one of the basic skills of banking.

Grade 2

For most people, promotion to Grade 2 comes after about six months. You may now be a standing order clerk, dealing with banker's orders and direct debits, making sure that a customer's mortgage or hire purchase payments go out on time.

You may be a cashier. As such you are an ambassador. The cashiers are the people most customers regularly see – they are the faces of the bank. Your job now becomes really personalized. The old lady and her foibles; the young man or woman who flirts with you and whose charm is fuller than their account; the misers; the worried; the serve-me-quick and let-me-go people; the manager of the supermarket where you shop – you'll meet a cross-section of the population.

As a more experienced Grade 2 you may be in charge of the counter

in a small branch, supervising other cashiers and controlling the
amount of cash held in the tills. Literally thousands of pounds may
pass through your hands daily. You may be put in charge of an
inquiry desk, helping customers with queries about their accounts
and dealing with basic questions about the bank's services.

Grade 3

After a couple of years of increasingly responsible clerical and customer contact work, it is possible to be promoted to Grade 3 duties.
In larger branches Grade 3 staff may be in charge of other cashiers
on the counter, or in charge of the back-office accounting section.
Normally, though, Grade 3 work is more technical. It can be as a
foreign clerk, handling foreign currency and travellers' cheques for
customers going on holiday, or for business customers trading
abroad. Grade 3 work may also involve some securities handling. As
a safe custody clerk, for instance, you may take responsibility for
handling customers' valuables deposited at the branch for safe keeping. You may arrange insurance cover for them, or get a stockbroker's
advice and act on their behalf to buy or sell shares. And you may be
involved in the preparation of documents for a customer who wants
to apply for a mortgage to buy a new house.

The work at Grade 3 is more technical than in the lower clerical
grades. But it is only at the next stage that staff become directly
involved for the first time in the central business of the banks –
lending.

Grade 4

0 Grade 4s are the most senior of the clerical staff in a bank, and their
1 work reflects that greater responsibility. Grade 4s will be experi-
2 enced in all the clerical work of a branch, and will have had the
3 theoretical framework for their more technical duties clearly
4 covered in the Institute of Bankers' courses that they will by now
5 have completed.
6   One of the key Grade 4 roles until now has been securities clerk.
7 In this job you are responsible for safeguarding the bank's money by
8 ensuring that the securities used to get loans are properly in order.

The loans will have been agreed and arranged at a higher level, but the securities become your responsibility. These securities can be insurance policies, stocks and shares, that kind of thing. The deeds to a home are rarely accepted these days, because no bank likes to repossess and make a borrower homeless. Deeds to a home are normally held only against mortgages.

The increasing use of standard forms for most personal loans has reduced the number of private-customer security-checking jobs, and this is one of the traditional bank branch functions that could, in time, become something of a rarity.

Also in Grade 4 are managers' clerks. This job is not only excellent training for management, but it can also be interesting and rewarding in itself, since it involves being, literally, the manager's assistant and taking the more routine work off his or her desk. Depending on the individual manager, there should also be some decision-taking, mainly on small loans and overdraft requests, and plenty of routine letter-answering and letter-writing.

The management structures differ a little from one bank to another, as do the actual job titles, but Grades 1 to 4 are for the most part known generally as the 'clerical grades'.

Management

After the clerical grades come supervisory or junior management posts, the 'appointed officers' of the banks. At this stage you may be sent to head office or to a regional office to work on a broader range of jobs. You learn to assess lending proposals submitted by branches within an area, and a lot more that will stand you in good stead for the managerial chair if and when you go back to branch banking.

If you do go back to the branches, the next step is as an assistant manager, or even as manager of a small branch. As a manager, you become solely responsible not only for the organization and administration of the branch, but also for its profitability.

You are now very much in the direct firing line of the customers, who will want to see you for loans, complaints, advice and general hand-holding. You cannot see everyone, and it would be idiotic for you to try, so you rely on your staff to handle some of the personal contacts.

In branch management at all levels you have to visit commercial and industrial customers at their places of operations to judge their loan-worthiness and their future promise, or otherwise. Customers at this stage will want advice on anything from tax to short- or longer-term loans and many other financial matters. You will not be expected to answer every question on the spot, but you will know where to find out what your customers want and need to know. Each manager, depending on seniority and size of branch, has strictly defined limits on how much he or she can lend before referring loan requests up the management hierarchy.

You will be expected to market and promote your bank's services. There are various ways of doing this, for example persuading existing account holders to use other services, such as insurance or extra personal loans. There is also the occasional chance to win a new customer. But most of these come by recommendation, and your best marketing ploy is to satisfy those customers you already have.

Being a manager is not a dead end job. There are bigger branches to go to, and beyond those are the head office departments. However, few branch bankers get beyond managerial posts; only a small percentage can rise to the very top.

What makes a manager? According to the banks themselves, common sense in abundance comes top, and commercial judgement only second. You need the commercial judgement; and you need a nose to smell out good or bad propositions, however well presented the nicely-cooked cash flow and balance sheet figures may be. You need to understand people, and you need to be able to get on with them.

For example, you may have to put on a hard hat and walk round construction sites, or talk to local surveyors and estate agents or other commercial and industrial contacts in order to learn about your customer companies and their potential, and to let them learn about your bank's services. 'Selling' is an increasingly important part of a manager's job.

You will certainly need to have passed the Institute of Bankers' exams. You will have undergone the bank's own training, and you will not be a manager until your bank's personnel staff, and your seniors, are quite convinced of your readiness for the job. Age and seniority alone are no guarantee of a branch of your own to run. At

every stage of your career there are constant performance and attitude assessments. Few businesses, in fact, take such care to ensure
that the people with potential for promotion get the chance to prove
their worth.

If you are the type to go into banking from personal choice, you
are almost certainly the type to like the job at its various stages. You
will say, as most managers do, that if you had to make the choice
you would do it all again.

But if you are at all in doubt, don't go into banking. Try for a job
that you are really sure you *want* to do. Job security isn't everything.

Secretarial Work

In most of the banks you can turn being a secretary into a career
rather than merely a job. New banking services are constantly being
introduced, and secretarial staff are increasingly in demand,
especially at head office and the main area offices.

Banks like you to have a minimum typing speed of 35 words per
minute. For bank work an accurate 35 wpm is much better than a 40
wpm with even one mistake. Shorthand should run to 80 wpm. You
should also be able to use audio equipment and a word-processor,
or be willing to be trained. You normally need at least O-level English, and you need to show some initiative – your job interview will
aim to find out if you have it.

Word-processors these days are easy to learn and, as there are
relatively inexpensive evening classes, it is a good idea to master at
least the rudiments and thus become a fast learner once you join the
bank. Once there, you will normally be sent on a special word-
processing and general secretarial course for 1–8 weeks.

You may start work in a branch – or you may get straight into a
head office department. Apart from the specialist training courses,
you will be expected to improve your speeds on the job without
losing accuracy.

One thing is unlikely – that you could move into operational banking from the secretarial stream. If you join a bank as a general clerical
trainee they say that there is no barrier to women achieving anything
that men can do – though there are some women who doubt that –

but don't think that starting as a secretary is the answer to promotion in other jobs.

Once a secretary, always a secretary. But the job can carry increased responsibility, and as you become more expert the people for whom you work may become more important. You may become a senior secretary, an indispensable ally to the senior management or even to a director on the main board of the bank. You need to be totally trustworthy, absolutely loyal, able to keep the most exciting secrets, and tactful to the ultimate degree about where your boss is, or what he or she is doing. As office technology advances, the secretary's role is rapidly changing. The boring paper-shuffling of the past is giving way to a far greater degree of electronic information-handling, and this is turning secretaries into genuine personal assistants to senior managers – the chief executive's secretary these days may wield more real power than most managers.

As a secretary you will be properly paid. Salaries start at between £3,500 and £4,500 a year on a scale rising to around £10,000, with extra pay for working in London or other big cities. If you are single and are required to move away from the parental home there will be relocation allowances.

Secretaries enjoy the same benefits as other banking staff – pension schemes, profit-sharing, free banking and other fringe benefits, as well as the out-of-hours social life.

2 Pay, Hours and Conditions

The salary structure of banking takes the form of a tall but sharply pointed pyramid. Down at the base there are tens of thousands of clerical, junior management and middle management staff earning respectable, but not exceptional, salaries. Towards the top of the pyramid there are several thousand senior managers in the high street banks and merchant banks, earning, on average, more than their contemporaries in industrial management. Right at the apex of the pyramid there are a very few senior men (and precious few women), either at the top of their career ladders in the big clearing banks or among the high flyers of the merchant banks, who earn internationally competitive salaries around and sometimes way beyond the £100,000 a year mark.

In an annexe to one side of this basic pay structure are the City of London investment banking and securities' house dealers – 'screen traders' – whose pay, with bonuses, may well be between £50,000 and £150,000 a year at the age of thirty or younger.

Even allowing for that pay pyramid peak, few people join a bank to make their fortune. Up to the middle salary ranges, promotion for the ambitious – particularly for graduate entrants, who are now given a flying start in the pace of their training and job opportunities – can fairly be planned. Beyond that, in the jobs paying £30,000 a year and above, competition becomes as fierce as the job opportunities become scarce. And this is a position that is unlikely to change, since the banks are becoming increasingly willing to appoint outside experts to take over specialist and highly paid work in the developing, non-traditional banking areas of the business – in marketing, advertising, sales promotion, computer systems development and investment.

For the average new entrant straight from school, basic salaries start in the £3,500–£4,500 range, depending on age and qualifications.

Salaries are reviewed annually. Graduate entrants benefit from a higher starting point on the pay grade structure because they are three, perhaps five, years older than the school-leavers. But they are also given an extra allowance for their academic qualifications, and their pay reflects the banks' willingness to match the market rate for the best of the degree crop. They can expect to start at between £6,000 and £7,500 a year, depending on the bank and the graduate entrant scheme they join.

Most of the banks operate a relatively rigid grade structure, with fourteen distinct pay groupings and more senior management grades beyond that.

The overwhelming majority of bank staff start, and remain, within the clerical grades 1 to 4. Secretarial staff, although they may have marginally different grading systems, also fall into this clerical group. In the 1–4 grades, salaries are within the following broad ranges: £3,500–£4,500; £4,500–£6,500; £6,500–£8,000; and up to a maximum basic clerical salary of between £8,500 and £10,500. Take-home pay in these grades can be boosted by age and seniority allowances, extra pay for academic qualifications, for additional responsibilities or for working in cities with special location supplements, plus overtime.

Above Grades 1–4 lie the lower reaches of assistant management, offering salaries from £9,000 to around £15,000 a year. Then come the junior management roles, in the £14,000 to £19,000–£20,000 range. Some of the managers of smaller bank branches come into this range, as do the assistant branch managers of more active offices, and the personal assistants to big branch managers or more senior bank executives.

Middle management in a bank may mean being in charge of a medium-sized branch, or taking one of the many administrative jobs in the banks' head offices, in their specialist departments, or in a subsidiary finance house or leasing company. Pay scales here range up from £17,500 or so into the mid £20,000s.

Recent pay surveys show that there are over thirty-five different banking jobs commanding salaries higher than the £21,000 average for managers in the British engineering industry; and over twenty jobs that offer more than the £26,000 average for engineering company directors. But these figures are slightly over-generous for bankers as a whole, because they include the concentration of high-earning international banking management based in the City. Still, successful bank managers will often be earning on a par with or above the average for most of their contemporaries in manufacturing industry.

After the middle management grades, in the very much thinner section of the pay pyramid – and in the early to late 40s for a successful career banker – there are the senior management jobs. A major bank branch or a division of the bank's specialist services to manage, or charge of a section of international business – these few thousand jobs across the industry take basic salaries up to and beyond £25,000 a year and, depending on age and the seniority of the post, to around £35,000–£42,500 on retirement.

Just a few hundred of these senior managers go on from there, often in their mid 40s or early 50s, into bank general managership. They may be put in charge of the bank's branches for an entire region, or may become an area director, responsible for all aspects of the bank's business in a particular part of the country. Salaries in these jobs can be at least £40,000 basic for the youngest of the high flyers, but will more likely be in the £50,000–£60,000-plus range.

Beyond those jobs the grade system begins to vanish in the clouds. Only a handful of a bank's general managers ever reach the very top. Quite a few senior managers in their mid 50s have to accept that they will never beat their contemporaries and their younger rivals to the top jobs, so they settle back and allow seniority steadily to top up their salaries and eventual pension rights. A few take early retirement, if they feel tired of the in-fighting which can happen at the top. A bare few decide to take up offers of outside directorships, become involved in new ventures beyond the banking halls, or take jobs with international banks, where they can pick up far better salaries in return for their reputation, experience and contacts.

Those who do win through to the top jobs in the high street banks are paid salaries that reflect the responsibility of managing some of the largest, and some of the most profitable, corporations in the world. However, British bank chiefs are, if anything, grossly under-paid in comparison with their colleagues in the United States or on the continent. A salary of over £100,000 a year in Britain looks decidedly more modest when the taxman has taken his cut, and it scarcely compares to the multi-million-dollar pay and share option schemes that US corporate banking chiefs have come to expect in return for far less secure contracts of employment.

Merchant and investment bankers, who tend to work in a more obviously internationally competitive world, take due note of the world rate for top quality bankers, those with the best business contacts and the wits to use them. There is no equivalent basic pay scale beyond the clerical offices of the merchant banks.

A top-flight international banker, in his or her late 30s or early 40s, can earn £150,000–£200,000 a year working in Hong Kong, New York, or elsewhere on the world money circuit. In the UK that salary would probably drop to around £85,000 for a British manager of that age and experience working in any of the 300 overseas bank offices, 160 bank representative offices, 200 foreign investment banks or 50-plus British-owned international or merchant banking houses based in and around the City of London. However, salary bonuses may 'top up' their pay to world rates.

As free marketeers, the merchant bankers also positively encourage their managements to build up outside directorships and to acquire personal wealth through share option schemes and other business interests, in a way that is totally at odds with the high street bankers' training and business culture. Senior merchant bankers, suffice it to say, do quite well on and off the pay scale.

For bank staff generally, basic pay is only one aspect of a broad and comfortable package of benefits. Each bank has its own individual package of 'fringe benefits', but many of the schemes are common to most of the major high street banks, and for full-time staff they generally include:

- *Free staff banking*. This generally includes an implied, or fairly clearly stated, condition that staff stay in credit. Random, unagreed overdrafts are frowned upon. Interest may be paid even on the current accounts of staff who stay in credit.
- *Low-cost bank loans*. As a rule these are most valuable for house purchase, where a 4–7 per cent interest rate is the usual flat-rate charge. There may be age restrictions on such a home loan (normally 23 for married staff and 25 for single staff). Any staff leaving the bank would have to

rearrange a mortgage in the open market straight away. Loans are normally up to a maximum of 95 per cent of a house or flat valuation unless the house move is occasioned by a posting, in which case loans can be 100 per cent of the value. Other low-cost loans tend to depend upon what the money is for. A car loan that the staff member can clearly afford to repay is one thing; a sizeable personal loan for some ill-defined, possibly frivolous, purpose will rarely be given. Staff are not usually allowed to borrow from other sources without prior permission.

– *Interest-free loans for season tickets.* Staff can use these to buy a quarterly or yearly season ticket for train, tube or bus, significantly reducing travel costs.

– *Removal cost allowance.* To help pay for a home move if this becomes necessary because of a job posting.

– *Big city allowances.* These are paid to staff in addition to their basic salaries. For example, in London the allowances in 1986 were:

	£ p.a.
Working within 3 miles of the centre	1,725
Working 3–6 miles out	1,223
Working 6–10 miles out	821
Working 10–16 miles out	654
Working 16–22 miles out	418

The 'centre', for the purpose of these calculations, is Charing Cross. An allowance of £289 a year is paid to staff working in most other major cities.

– *Lodging allowances.* Paid to younger staff who have to rent accommodation because of a job move.

– *Pension schemes.* Usually non-contributory; in a few instances they may cost 5 per cent of salary. Bank pensions are normally based on a scale that runs to a maximum of $^{40}/_{60}$ of your final salary. This is comparable to pension arrangements for staff in most of the service industries these days, and means retiring on a maximum of two-thirds of your final salary if you serve a full 40 years. The retirement age for new entrants across the industry, men and women, is being harmonized at 60.

- *Annual bonus.* In recent years this has become a standard 2½ per cent of basic salary, paid in December. The money is not counted as pensionable pay, nor is it regarded either as subject to union negotiation or, although it is becoming a hard-to-break tradition, as a right.

- *Profit-sharing schemes.* These vary year by year depending upon the individual bank's profit performance. In the highly profitable major high street bank these schemes have been worth between 4 and 7 per cent of basic salary in the last 10 years. Most banks now allow staff to receive their profit-sharing allowance in the form of shares rather than cash. There may also be a savings-related share option scheme to enable staff to acquire their bank's shares in a fast, efficient, low-cost way.

- *Company cars.* These are reserved for managers on the higher grades, or for managers who can justify high mileage in their districts. Banking staff complain that they are falling behind industrial managers in the provision of this tax efficient 'perk'.

- *Expense accounts.* These are not generous by other service industry standards, and tend to be wrapped tightly with red tape in the high street banks. Merchant bankers above the clerical grades have distinctly more lavish facilities.

- *Lunch facilities.* Most of the big bank offices have greatly discounted canteen facilities, and staff away from these facilities may, depending on the bank, have an allowance to match the bigger-office lunch savings.

- *Medical insurance.* Most of the major banks have membership of group medical schemes, which provide private health care for staff and, in most instances, low-cost arrangements to include families in the scheme.

In addition, bank staff have come to expect that their employers abide scrupulously by all the current legislation covering conditions of employment. The Factories and Offices laws, which determine the facilities available for staff at work, the proper provision of lighting, heating and so forth, are strictly adhered to.

Although many bank staff have to put up with working in buildings converted to uses for which they were not initially designed, and others may find that their working space has become cramped with the addition of new cash-handling equipment, computer terminals, and the space-eating 'bandit screens' that protect counter staff, banks, as a whole, have a reputation for providing some of the best working accommodation in the service industries.

Banks also tend to apply not just the letter but very much the spirit of employment law. For example, full-time staff are granted maternity leave from the eleventh week before the expected birth and, after the full statutory time away from work, they have the right to return to a job with the same grade. Some banks further extend this principle to allow mothers to return to a same-grade job after an absence of a couple of years; and most now also allow a period of unpaid leave for staff who are adopting children.

Paternity leave has yet to be accepted as a staff right by most banks. But only in exceptional circumstances would any bank prevent a staff member from taking holiday time in those cases.

Women who leave the bank to have children are able to maintain their right to low-cost home loans only if they intend to return to work full-time. And if staff having children mistime their efforts and are away from work over the winter months, they may lose their annual bonus and profit-sharing money.

Holidays for most bank staff run from a minimum of 21 days a year to a maximum of 30 days, depending on seniority. This excludes 8 annual bank holidays.

Overtime working is a constant source of bank staff discussion. Normally, clerical staff in Grades 1 to 4 are paid overtime for every half an hour worked beyond the 9 to 5 basic day – a standard 35-hour, 5-day week (or 32-hour, 4½-day week in the case of the TSB). Weekend working is generally paid at a higher than weekday overtime rate – but each bank operates a different scheme. Managerial staff above these grades do not generally qualify for overtime – their rights to overtime are 'bought out' with a cash payment on reaching appointed officer grades, or a particular salary level. In any case, there is a long tradition of voluntary overtime – branch staff clear backlogs of work out of normal hours, and managers take work home. The banking unions argue that unpaid overtime, while it may be understandable when staff are involved in some project, or are trying to keep their branch up to the mark, is one of the reasons why the banks are able to mask understaffing.

The banks normally insist on having a clear right to be able to post staff to any branch or office within the United Kingdom. There are complex arrangements for staff to appeal to be exempted from a proposed move, and clerical grade staff are less likely to be moved out of their home area than those in the higher grades. Secretarial staff in the larger offices rarely have to face a move, although the relocation of a number of big 'back office' departments out of Central London has, in recent years, involved staff in all grades having to choose between a move and leaving their bank.

Most of the management training schemes operated by the banks include a 2- or 3-year period of experience in a number of different branches and head office departments. During training these bankers may have to move two, three or more times. Later in their careers managers' moves become less frequent, although the route to senior management in the high street banks generally zigzags across the country from branch to department, and from region to head office, as the manager moves on to progressively more responsible jobs.

3 Training for the Job

Bankers, like all professionals, spend much of their careers training for the next task. From the first day in a bank there are practical banking procedures to learn. Throughout a banking career, in branches, in administrative offices, or in subsidiary companies, there will always be new areas of responsibility to prepare for, new customer requests to handle, and, increasingly, new equipment and new methods of dealing with banking business to come to grips with. Even after 20, 30 or 40 years' work in a bank, experience alone is not enough. There are refresher courses to attend, and there are always additional technical training schemes to help staff keep abreast of changing financial services.

Right up to the end of their banking career, when pre-retirement planning courses start to look interesting, bankers can be, and generally are, training.

Just how much training and how many professional qualifications are needed depends on the ambitions of the individual.

Clerical staff who have no career horizon beyond counter work, or who would be happy enough spending their days in a typing pool, are not expected to cover their walls with banking certificates. For them, the training systems of all the banks are fairly similar: on-the-job working experience is backed up by local management assessments and by a clear set of clerical training procedures, aimed to ensure that all staff are able to handle the full range of jobs in their grade.

It is for the would-be management trainees that the comprehensive and more academic training programmes are designed. And at the heart of all these training schemes lie the examination courses of the Institute of Bankers, and the Institute of Bankers in Scotland.

The Institute of Bankers was founded in London in 1879, in the earliest days of the career bankers. It is a professional body with 110,000 members worldwide. Like its fellow professional body north of the border, its aims are primarily educational.

Just how actively a bank promotes the idea of Institute examinations to staff depends on the pace of the training programme they join.

At one extreme, the cream of the graduate entrants might join an accelerated promotion scheme tailored for future senior management, which could involve a crash course in banking fast enough to take them through the first level of Institute examinations within 18 months, and through the entire range of Institute courses inside 3–4 years.

At the other end of the scale, it is more likely that entrants will be gently encouraged to take an interest in professional qualifications after a few years in the bank. If they prove to be enthusiastic about Institute courses, they may get their local manager's backing for an application for day-release study time or other in-house training facilities, enabling them to take the Institute examinations at their own pace.

Institute of Bankers courses fall into 3 progressively harder layers.

The first layer consists of introductory courses designed for school-leavers with O- and A-level qualifications, or their Scottish equivalent Highers, or those with adequate CSE passes at O grade. Only those with the equivalent of 4 Os, including English and one quantitive subject, such as mathematics, may enter for the Institute examinations. That's why the banks tend to ask for 4 Os as their minimum entry qualification these days.*

The introductory courses cover basic accountancy, background information on banking, and a preliminary look at commercial law. Graduates with a recognized degree are exempt from these Stage 1 courses. But most graduates need to familiarize themselves with the course material if they are to make sense of the later stages of the Institute courses, unless their degree has included commercial subjects in some form.

In cases where graduate entrants have completed a degree in a

---

* After 1988, the O-level GCE examination will cease to exist as such. It will be replaced by the new GCSE examination.

specifically commercial subject, there are additional exemptions from parts of the second layer, the Institute Diploma courses.

These second stage courses cover more detailed work on the law and practice of banking, on economics, and on the basic elements of business accounting. In these, as in other Institute courses, the work tends to be a mixture of recent historical background reading, case law, and case studies. It is not dissimilar, in fact, to first-year degree work. But the courses do lack the face-to-face interaction of lectures or seminars. Students will have colleagues who have completed the courses, and they may have contact with other members of study groups to discuss the material. Otherwise they are learning at a distance, from text books, by the study of model answers, and by broader reading around the subjects.

The Diploma course goes on to more detailed money and banking studies, and more technical business accounting. It also embraces basic investment theory, more complex areas of banking law and practice, elements of management theory, and international banking.

Beyond the Diploma examinations are the Associateship courses. Only the more academically minded junior staff and the promotion-conscious management trainees enrol for these higher qualifications. The courses here range across even more technical aspects of banking, covering in some detail such areas as management and business administration, specialist management accounting and business finance and taxation, together with yet more banking law and practice.

There are separate Institute courses for those specializing in international banking or in legal trustee work. There are also an increasing number of even more specialist banking qualifications beyond the Institute Diploma and Associateship examinations. The Financial Studies Diploma (Dip. FS), for instance, is a degree-level qualification in banking and management sponsored by the Institute. There are also banking and finance degree-level qualifications in banking and management sponsored by the Institutes. Loughborough University of Technology has degree courses in banking and finance, and similar banking-based degree courses are run at a number of business schools.

An increasing number of the accelerated promotion graduates find that their initial years of training don't end there. After a few extra years in their bank, the best of the crop may find themselves dispatched to business schools to complete a Masters of Business Administration (MBA) course.

In all cases, from the basic Institute introductory courses upwards, banks encourage their staff to work for professional qualifications by rewarding examination success with extra pay.

Far up the promotion ladder, another round of academic 'training' takes place – this forms part of the sorting process that selects the senior managers who will rise to the very top jobs. The 40- to 50-year-old 'high flyers' take a few months out from their jobs to attend senior executive refresher courses at business schools around the world. There they meet the heirs apparent of major corporations from every country and every type of industry. Whether these 'training' courses are seen as involving morning to night study, or treated as a relaxed sabbatical by an exotic gold course, rather depends upon the confidence of these top 'trainees'.

You can find out more about the Institute banking examinations, and get details of the education exemptions from parts of courses, by writing to one of the following:

> The Institute of Bankers
> Emanuel House
> 4–9 Burgate Lane
> Canterbury CT1 2XJ

> The Institute of Bankers in Scotland
> 20 Rutland Square
> Edinburgh EA1 2DE

Institute Qualifications

1. *The Institute of Bankers*

The examinations are in two stages:

Stage 1. The object of Stage 1 courses is to provide sufficient grounding in basic commercial studies to enable candidates to undertake Stage 2, and details are as follows:

Stage 1 course

BTEC National Award in Business and Finance (Finance Core) to include the following options:

Year 1 – Elements of Banking 1

Year 2 – Elements of Banking 2

Entry requirements: 4 O-levels or equivalent including English language

1 Year Institute of Bankers' Conversion course which covers:

Economics

Accounts

Law

Elements of Banking or Elements of Investment (for candidates intending to take the Trustee Diploma)

Entry requirements: 1 or more A-levels plus O-level or equivalent in English language

Methods of study available:

1. College courses for which day-release may be granted.
2. Correspondence courses.

Stage 2. Career bankers will wish to continue their studies and achieve Associateship of the Institute of Bankers. The length of time required to complete the Diploma will depend upon the individual, but with good progress it should take about 3 years. Successful completion of the Stage 2 examinations, together with 3 years' banking service and 3 years' Institute membership, qualifies for the award of Associateship (AIB).

There are three routes to the AIB: the Banking, International Banking or Trustee Diploma. The majority of bankers take the Banking Diploma.

Stage 2 course (Banking Diploma)

Part A Law relating to Banking

Monetary Economics

Accountancy

Part B Investment

Nature of Management

Finance of International Trade
Part C Practice of Banking 1 and 2
Entry requirements: Stage 1 qualification or recognized
university degree

Methods of study available:
1. Tuition is available at approximately 150 colleges in
   England and Wales
2. Correspondence courses

Financial Studies Diploma. This is a degree level course designed
for those expected to reach senior management.

Content
Practice of Banking 3, 4 and 5
Human Aspects of Management
Business Planning and Control
Marketing of Financial Services
Entry requirements: Banking, International Banking or
Trustee Diploma or recognized degree or professional
qualifications

2. The Institute of Bankers in Scotland

Initial Stage

Introductory course
The course provides an introduction to the subjects of:
Accounting
Banking
Commercial Law
Minimum qualifications for entry – four H grades or three
H grades plus two O grades or equivalent (i.e. two A-levels
plus two O-levels). English at H grade or A-level must be
included.

or

Scottish National Certificate in Business Studies
Those who do not hold the necessary H grade or A-level

passes to take the Introductory Course require to complete this Certificate.

Minimum qualifications for entry are 4 SCE O grades or equivalent, including English.

Diploma Course. Examinations leading to the award of the Diploma of the Institute of Bankers in Scotland – Dip. IB (Scot.)

> Year 1 Law and Practice of Banking I
> Economics
> Business Accounting
> Year 2 Money and Banking
> Business Accounting II
> Investment
> Year 3 Law and Practice of Banking II
> Foreign Business

Associate Course.   Examinations taken after one year of study leading to the award of the Associateship of the Institute of Bankers in Scotland – AIB (Scot.)

> Management and Business Administration
> Management Accounting and Business Finance
> Taxation

4 The Banking Unions

Because many bank staff work in small groups alongside their own local branch management, there is not the tradition of mass union membership which is common in factory-based industries. Nevertheless, in recent years the banking unions have expanded in size and influence, and they have effectively absorbed the banks' own staff associations, which were established as a compromise between the need for some form of broad staff representation and the early hostility of senior bank managements to trade unionism. These unions are increasingly able to make their voices heard on conditions of employment, pay, and staff changes to meet new developments in banking.

The banking unions have their roots in the organizations of bank clerks in England and Scotland which were formed in 1917 and 1919. The Bank Officers' Guild and the Scottish Bankers' Association came together in 1946 to form the National Union of Bank Employees. In 1971 NUBE changed its name to become today's Banking Insurance and Finance Union (BIFU). Around half of BIFU's 157,000 members work for the high street banks. Although clerical grade staff make up the core of the membership, a fair number of middle managers have stayed with the union as their careers have progressed. Their membership adds weight to the union's bargaining power, but it also acts as a moderating influence when it comes to discussing action to press for pay deals or improved service agreements. The rest of BIFU's membership comes from similar staff groups in insurance companies and building societies.

BIFU is now one of the top 20 unions by size within the Trades Union Congress (TUC). But it is consciously non-political. On and off merger talks between BIFU and its nearest rival, the Clearing Bank Union, have prevented staff having a single voice in union–management negotiations across the industry.

The other major union in the banking world, however, does take an openly political stance. The Association of Scientific, Technical and Managerial Staffs (ASTMS) has, under its general secretary Clive Jenkins, grown into one of the largest white-collar unions in Britain.

An active programme of expansion throughout the 1960s and 1970s brought many of the more union-conscious banking groups under the ASTMS banner. And that membership drive led to regular complaints of 'poaching' by the longer-established unions.

ASTMS's major step into the banking business dates from 1973, when the Midland Bank's staff association joined. The Clydesdale Bank's staff association followed their parent group into the union, along with the technical services staffs of the Midland and a number of other smaller groups of technical or professional staff within the banks. The evident enthusiasm for ASTMS's more active style of union representation among bank computer staff led to many warnings by senior management about the dangers of a handful of union members being able to 'hold the country to ransom'. Bank chiefs warned that union members could switch off the computers needed to keep Britain's banking system operating, and that the whole economy would be at the mercy of these few strikers.

In fact, none of the banking unions has ever mounted a successful strike. Occasional threats of industrial action form part of the regular negotiation process, and membership ballots have, on occasion, produced majority votes in favour of overtime bans. But the banking unions accept that, on the whole, their members are not militant unionists.

Much of the work of the bank unions in the recent past has been connected with monitoring job security agreements and improving the lot of women staff. BIFU, the Clearing Bank Union, and ASTMS campaign for positive discrimination to improve the career prospects of female staff.

Although 55 per cent of bank staff are women, a disproportionate percentage of those are employed in the lower clerical grades, working at branch counters or handling non-managerial paperwork in branches and administrative offices. Even today, when banks do hold jobs for women who leave to have children, and are publicly committed to being 'equal opportunity employers', only a very few women break through into senior management.

BIFU pursues a particularly active health and safety policy. The union has successfully campaigned to change working practices so that branch staff are less exposed to danger from bank robbers. Trained security guards rather than clerks now handle cash movement in and out of branches. And union pressure has speeded the introduction of bandit-proof screens, which separate counter staff handling cash from public areas.

Another area of union activity has been less successful, however. The unions oppose the compulsory mobility clauses in the banks' contracts of employment. In theory, these mobility clauses give the banks the right to direct a member of staff from one branch to another at short notice. In practice, the banks do not normally insist on a move without fairly full discussion, but, for anyone looking for promotion in a bank, mobility is regarded as essential. Turning down a job move for whatever reason may mean being passed over for promotion on another occasion. And, in the managerial grades, staff often have to weigh the disruption involved in moving house, transferring children to new schools, and cutting into a partner's career, against the opportunity of a better job.

The unions have managed to improve the amount of consultation between management and staff over moves; but they have had little success in persuading banks to advertise branch vacancies internally so as to allow those who do want to move to apply.

On basic pay, the unions have pressed hard for increases that reflect the profitability of the banks and the increased productivity of employees as they have adapted to new technology. They have been anxious to preserve the 'perks' their members have accumulated over the years: the low-cost home loans, free staff banking and annual bonus payments. The banks, however, tend to regard such extra benefits, particularly the profit-sharing and bonus schemes, as non-negotiable. They resist being committed to these extra pay schemes regardless of profitability, and refuse to include even regular bonus deals in basic, pensionable pay.

Bank staff's standard 35-hour week is already in line with the target set by the Trades Union Congress for all industries. And although the bank unions have regularly campaigned for even shorter working hours – formally calling for a 28-hour, 4-day working week – it is only recently, with the reopening of bank branches on Saturdays, that this working week debate has become a real cause of union–management conflict.

The mixture of voluntary overtime agreements (disliked by the unions) and negotiated settlements between staff and management explains the patchy way in which Saturday banking has reappeared in Britain.

BIFU managed to negotiate a basic 32-hour, 4½-day working week for staff at the Trustee Savings Bank, plus extra pay and some 600 new jobs when it settled terms for Saturday opening. That has become the new yardstick for union negotiations with the rest of the industry.

Branch staff on duty on Saturdays are supported by a mass of automatic cash withdrawal and deposit equipment. The machines take care of the time-consuming work of money-handling, and leave staff free to deal with customer queries about loans and other bank services.

Moves towards automated banking, while making the Saturday opening of branches more acceptable to staff, are a major long-term concern of the unions.

The unions' heavy concentration of membership among clerical grades within the banks makes them particularly sensitive to developments that could eliminate many of the more mundane jobs in the industry. Until now, the growth of demand for banking services has been such that job numbers have continued to increase despite the banks' massive investment in new equipment. No one expects that to continue indefinitely, and BIFU estimates that further automation could cut the number of jobs in banking by as much as 12 per cent (around 50,000 jobs) over the next 10 years.

Clive Jenkins of ASTMS recognized the possible impact of new technology on staff numbers in his book *The Collapse of Work*, written with the union's then director of research Barrie Sherman in 1979. In it he considered the outlook for white-collar industries into the next century, and outlined the policies that have become an increasing part of the banking unions' stance on job futures.

The unions favour earlier voluntary retirements, and they have

welcomed the banks' increasing willingness to accept early retirement applications. Across the industry the normal retirement age is
being equalized at 60 for men and women.

Unions have also campaigned, without much success, to have staff
negotiations and prior agreement on the introduction of all new
equipment. Calls on BIFU members to refuse to operate new equipment unless it was introduced as part of a wider package of negotiations on job security have as yet failed to win widespread support.

The banking unions are conscious of the potential threat to jobs
posed by new technology. But the non-militance of their membership means that no serious efforts have been made to challenge the
banks' move towards increasing automation. Most bank staff have,
in fact, welcomed new equipment, regarding it as necessary in order
to cut down on the mountains of repetitive paperwork, and essential
if their banks are to keep up with the rest of the high street competition.

The unions have been careful not to create situations where the
loyalty of staff to their bank and to their union is brought too sharply
into contest. The banks for their part have been increasingly careful
not to create unnecessary conflict with unionized staff. In a long
period of growth, both in staff numbers and in bank profitability, this
mutual caution has ensured a remarkably good industrial relations
record.

5 Social Life

It is worth repeating that there is little point in going for a career solely because it offers security, good pensions or cheap mortgages. You need to be sure that you will also enjoy the life, that you will get along in banking. There is no point in trying it unless you really can convince yourself in all honesty that you are the right type for the job. If you are unsure, forget it. You might end up being depressed or frustrated, and what good are fringe benefits then? Earn your pleasure as well as your pensions. And there is a certain attitude, a definable character, a type that is right for a career in banking.

You will need to admire and have respect for discipline, law and order; to be as honest as the day is long; to have integrity; to be ready to accept what is handed out and to make the best of it, because you will not always have a free choice. You may, for instance, become a manager but not be able to choose your own branch; and, even if you are lucky enough to work within a broad area that suits you, it may not be for very long. Some promotions may be to a bank up the road; others to an inconveniently distant one.

When you are a manager you will not really be able to choose your own staff, though you will certainly have some say about who you need, about the ability of those who are drafted to you, and about the way they either do, or don't, get on with their colleagues in the branch. A manager can recommend removal or promotion, and his opinions will be listened to because he knows what he is talking about.

Although as a manager you will carry a good deal of responsibility, you will rarely find a job in which you are the sole boss, even right at the top. Banks tend to make a great play about their need for the individual, for people with responsibility and initiative, but they are corporations that in fact rely upon the team spirit more than most. Systems are there or are created to be followed – perhaps improved upon – but never to be ignored or undermined. There are systems for everything, including promotion. Banks have a promotion ladder that has to be climbed, often slowly, mostly rung by rung; but never ever, as that sexy actress put it, 'wrong by wrong'.

Rank is very important in banking. In the branch you all work together, use each other's first names and often socialize together. But rank is paramount, and bankers learn never to treat their seniors other than as seniors. There's no need to touch your forelock or click your heels, but there is a need to know your place. When career bankers meet it doesn't take them long to work out within a millimetre each other's grade and seniority, and to act accordingly.

Even junior staff are allowed to criticize the system and the way things are done, as long as such criticism really is constructive and objective. Indeed, you will be seen as keen and observant if you make the right comments; but do it through the system, through your immediate boss. For example, you may be very knowledgeable about altering or adding to computer systems; someone else may think up some short cuts on customer service behind the scenes; another may be hot on cost-saving ideas. All such suggestions will be genuinely welcomed – you are supposed to be an intelligent individual, and there will be no objection to your proving it. In any case, anything that improves the way business is done will be welcome.

Out of working hours everyone is a free agent – up to a point. The restrictions that apply by day, at work, apply equally at night. You cannot be a banker by day and a soccer hooligan by night. Jekyll gets along very well in a bank. Hyde is soon found out and possibly expelled.

If you like your social life neatly laid out for you, with leisure pursuits there for the taking, you will find that the banks offer excellent opportunities for almost any kind of sport or creative arts and crafts through the countless bank and inter-bank societies. If you are a society-joiner and like the people you meet, you can enjoy an active leisure and social life at a high standard but at reasonable cost.

One of the reasons why banks are so good at these out-of-hours activities is the need for mobility of branch staff. When a person has to make perhaps half-a-dozen moves during his career, it is not easy to build up a social life in any one area; bank links can provide a quick and easy way of making new friends in new places.

Getting to know colleagues may also be a short cut to promotion. Social contacts can provide excellent stepping stones as well as good friends. A young banker, if he is able, will certainly climb the promotion ladder in the end, but there is no harm in being noticed through social activities. Play the right games with the right people, be that golf, bowls or dramatic art, and you will be very much a part of the working team as well. Banks have good personnel departments and keep excellent records and assessments of their staff, but knowing a senior who can add a personal appraisal to the bank's file can be a considerable help to any career.

Those who don't join in the bank's social activities may meet surprisingly few colleagues. A branch is rarely large, and you will not make many acquaintances there – even in departments outside the branch you may find yourself meeting at a friendly level only those on similar grades. The number of potential friends from work is thus reduced to a handful. This is far less of a potential problem for those with secretarial, clerical or specialist jobs at headquarters and area offices, but in a branch the range is restricted, and those week-end and evening activities and friends become important.

Because so many people go into banking when young, there is a high incidence of early marriage. For one thing, cheap mortgages for either partner make it much easier for them to buy a home than for other young people. There are also all those social meetings out of hours that we have just been talking about.

In the past, a banking lady who became a wife often had to settle for being part of her husband's background. Her own promotion chances tended to be affected in the event of pregnancy, because although she would be able to return to the bank without loss of seniority after having the baby, she might well have missed out on a few potential promotions in the meantime. And again, a married woman tends to be less able to fulfil the mobility requirements, unless she and her husband have the good luck to be posted to the same place every time. Of course, these days it is not always the husband who moves and the wife who follows – many couples make their own private decisions about which career move to follow.

Some even manage to live temporarily, even for years, in separate homes, getting together at week-ends and for holidays.

Banking wives rarely enter the business scene. They may appear at branch functions and parties, but seldom at the more general functions that bankers get invited to. Once above a certain management grade, however, bank managers are expected to bring their wives along. However, some wives, after spending so long in the background, find it difficult to adjust to a more public life when their husbands become senior managers. Once across that socially acceptable grade threshold many wives, not having been invited to business functions before, fear such occasions or stay away. It's easy enough for any man to sacrifice his wife to his career but, in banking with its particularly rigid promotion grades, it is often that much easier.

If you don't like an ordered social life, think again about whether you are the right person for the job in the first place. In all banks there are people who have made it to the top despite remaining highly individual, but they are always considered to have 'made good' because of their ability and *despite* being mavericks. On the whole, you have more chance of success as one of the herd. Just a little individuality is often enough to help you get on.

We all like to present an image to the world and, as a banker, that image will invariably be acceptable anywhere. Bankers are regarded as diligent, intelligent, honest, disciplined – who could quarrel with such virtues? All right, so you may be teased about the job and its safe, dull image, but rather less than, say, income tax inspectors are teased. The world still thinks of bankers as people counting banknotes behind iron bars, whatever the banks do to alter that picture in the public mind. The wide range of jobs available in banking, and the ever-increasing, interesting variety of behind-the-scenes work, are only vaguely known and understood by the public.

Bankers dress soberly. That's the image, but it is also still largely the fact. Male staff will wear a suit, or at least a suit-style jacket, with a shirt and tie, females a neat dress, blouse-and-skirt or ladies' suit. You will dress that way not because you are told to, but because that is what everyone else does. Don't let it worry you – every career has its uniform. The tattered jeans in the film/video/TV business, the leather jackets of art directors in advertising agencies and the exotic plumage of showbiz – all these are uniforms in their way, every bit as much as the conservative suit.

Bankers, especially branch bankers who meet the customers daily, are expected always to be smiling and polite, even when they are suffering screaming headaches, bitter marital rows, divorce, separation or bereavement. If you cannot play Pagliacci, tell your boss and ask for some time off to recover. You will get sympathy, understanding and leave of absence, but you will have to hide that aching or breaking heart when you come back again. Customers judge their banks by the façade and the people behind it. However, since that applies to just about everyone in all walks of life, it isn't really too much to expect.

6 As Others See Them

At the beginning of 1984 a slim but important book called *Banking Services and the Consumer* came on the banking scene. This was a report by the National Consumer Council (NCC), based on nation-wide interviews with many banks and building societies and on research to find out what customers really thought about their banks. It gave the consumer's view of banking, whether or not the consumer had a bank account.

During the couple of years it took to complete that investigation the banks did a great deal to extend their services to customers, and much of the recommended action had already been taken, or was in the pipeline, by the time the book was published. For example, the Banking Ombudsman – who will act as referee in disputes between banks and their customers – has been appointed, and it will be interesting to see how he fares. Other recommendations have not been taken up. The banks, for instance, still tend to take customers' money for bank charges without asking or warning, and account statements are still often hard to understand.

The National Consumer Council's recommendations are repeated verbatim here, and help to give an impression of the range of problem areas in bank services seen by the consumer organizations.

Recommendations to the banks

* We strongly welcome the development of interest-bearing current accounts which credit customers with the interest their money has earned and debit them with the charges for the work done on their behalf. We support charging systems which make it clear to consumers what they are paying for. We believe that, if our recommendations for encouraging competition in money transmission services are followed, such accounts should become more general. So far as current account practice is concerned we recommend that

    (i) banks should not take money for charges out of customers' accounts without telling them first;

(ii) banks should radically improve the way in which charges are presented to customers.

* All informal agreements on bank opening hours should cease. We welcome the gradual break-down in the standard pattern of bank hours, which many bank customers find inadequate.

* All automated teller machines and future point-of-sale equipment should give a printed record of transactions.

* Banks should give their customers better information about the costs of overdraft. They should inform customers of the annual percentage rate, calculated to a mutually agreed formula, when agreeing an arranged overdraft. They should also draw attention to the costs involved, when writing to customers about unarranged overdrafts.

* Banks should give all new customers opening current or deposit accounts a simple, attractively designed statement outlining the rights and obligations which customers have.

* Banks should inform all customers about the way their system for giving references on customers works. Customers should have the option to request the permission being sought whenever a reference is made to a banker. If this service imposes extra costs on the banks, banks should be able to charge for it, provided of course that this has been made clear to the customer.

* Bank customers should have access to factual records about the operation of their account.

* Banks should improve their internal procedures for dealing with trustee and executor work.

* The banks should collectively make arrangements for the creation and servicing of a Banking Ombudsman comparable to the Insurance Ombudsman. The Ombudsman should be empowered to consider and adjudicate upon all complaints of a personal banking nature, including executor and trust business, and should be requested to make and publish annual reports.

* The Scottish clearing banks should consider offering their customers opening hours which will serve them at least as well as banks serve their customers in England and Wales.

Recommendations to other organizations

* The Building Societies Association should cease to recommend interest rates to its members. It if does not, the exemption it enjoys from restrictive practices legislation should be withdrawn.

* No changes are necessary in the control of advertisements for savings. However the Independent Broadcasting Authority (IBA) and Advertising Stadards Authority (ASA) should continue to

scrutinize such advertisements carefully, and ASA should moni-
tor them on a regular basis.
* Financial advertising on satellite television and on cable should
meet the standards set by the IBA and ASA.

(from *Banking Services and the Consumer*, a report by the National Consumer Council)

In its survey of customers' attitudes the National Consumer Council's report gives an interesting insight into the public image of banks
and bankers. The report showed that customers were less displeased
about mistakes in their statements (almost everyone had at least one
experience of error) than they were about branch opening hours.
They felt that banks were not open to serve them when they wanted.

The banks tried projects such as late evening opening, but except
in Scotland, where some evening banking schemes continue, they
attracted too few customers to make the policy viable. Now the major
high street banks are reopening many branches on Saturday mornings. Whether 'bankees , as customers are coming to be called, will
use these Saturday services is not yet proven. But building societies
take a lot of savings and handle a good deal of business on Saturdays,
so competition has forced at least a trial of Saturday opening.

The survey confirmed that lunchtime queues were a bone of con-
tention. Innumerable customers resented finding half the tills in the
bank closed while the counter staff lunched at the times most people
are free to get to the counters. They felt that bank staff could lunch
at any time, but their own chances to get to the bank were restricted.

Bank charges, or rather the poor definition of them in account
statements, are another source of frustration and disgruntlement.
The NCC report showed that bank charges themselves are grudg-
ingly accepted, although customers are keenly appreciative of free
banking schemes.

Emotionally, the banks came off badly. The report shows that in
customers' eyes haughty attitudes, unfriendly service and a kind of
finger-wagging mentality are all generally attributed to individual
bank staff at all levels. Many customers feel distinctly ill at ease,
often in fear or awe of banks and rarely comfortable. As one of the
people questioned for the NCC report said, 'They've got your money
and they've used it how they like, they don't do you a favour.' Those
who like banks or found them approachable were those who had

established a relationship with someone helpful, and that was by no means always the manager.

There was a widespread feeling among customers that there was one standard of service for the rich and another for the poor: '. . . very aloof. If you're in business OK, but if you're "man in the street" no.' Customers wanted to be treated as equals, as deserving of consideration; although it must be admitted that many customers, it seems, would be happy to settle for pleasantness from the counter clerks. Not everyone wants to see the manager, or other senior officials of their branch. Indeed, many customers not only don't want such service, but feel that they would never need it.

What came over very strongly in the NCC research is the tremendous importance of all bank personnel being friendly with customers. Names on the counter are appreciated, but a smile, a 'thank you', a pleasant manner, combine to make every counter clerk who manages that their bank's best ambassador. A great many customers are still relatively unfamiliar with banks and banking and need to be put at ease to be reassured. They do not automatically understand banking and, especially, the technology of banking.

As customers come to understand the system, and use it, attitudes change. A few years ago customer dissatisfaction was chiefly focused on what were seen as haughty or condescending attitudes and manners. As people have become more familiar with banking, the personalities of the staff they deal with are regarded as less important than the quality of service, and customers become increasingly intolerant of inefficiency or errors. It is clearly important for any branch to keep down the number of errors, because the entire banking group is judged by them. Annoyingly for the bank, an error is an error, and one small one looms as large in the customer's mind as some heinous mistake.

Advertising can be a trap for the banks. When the Midland Bank advertised itself as the 'Listening Bank' it put itself in the firing line for customers, who hurried to write to the newspapers any time there seemed to be evidence to the contrary. If an advertisement shows smiling counter clerks, the first one who fails to raise a smile is taken as proof that the bank is unpleasant, even uncaring.

Not everyone opens a bank account from choice. Companies which pay wages or salaries straight into banks have been responsible for recruiting more account customers than any come-hither advertising or promotions on the part of the bank. These customers probably did not come too reluctantly but, since they were not volunteers but conscripts, the banks have had to remind their staff that it is important not to treat them as a captive audience. Staff must recognize that these customers still need courtship if they are to learn to enjoy having their bank accounts and to use bank services as frequently as possible.

The banks spend tens of millions of pounds each year working to improve their public image. Community affairs projects can be anything – a local branch's contribution towards the village scout hut, or secondment of a bank manager to a national charity to help sort out its finances. Arts and sports sponsorship keeps the individual bank's name in the public eye, and it helps to link the bank with the kinds of activity it thinks that its customers, or its prospective customers, would approve of. So blood sports are given a wide berth, but good, safe, thoroughly British activities like cricket are considered appropriate. Motor racing for those banking businesses most interested in providing car loan finance; cash for student rags for the campus bankers; prizes for business initiative awards with an eye on small company development finance . . . all these items of selective generosity have their role in promoting the bank's image.

Customer complaints to banks tend to be responded to with excessive zeal. When customers write to a bank chairman with a complaint about a local branch's failure to be helpful, layer upon layer of bank administration swings into action to ensure that the customer gets a satisfactory answer, or an apology. The banks have learned that these days customers are increasingly willing to move their accounts to other banks if they are unhappy with the service they receive, or if they think that their complaints are being ignored.

Bank recruitment programmes lay heavy emphasis on the need to be outgoing, helpful and friendly with customers. In an increasingly competitive market that attitude has never been more important.

What Customers Think of Banks

Overall, how satisfied or dissatisfied are you with the service you receive from your bank?

	%
Very satisfied	62
Fairly satisfied	30
Neither satisfied nor dissatisfied	3
Fairly dissatisfied	4 ⎫ 5
Very dissatisfied	1 ⎭

Analysis (Base)	Percent dissatisfied
All (1284)	5
Age: 15-24 (172)	10
25-34 (283)	7
35-44 (276)	6
45-54 (181)	4
55-65 (207)	3
65+ (165)	1
Bank charges: paid in last 12 months (567)	7
not paid (533)	4
Errors made: in last 12 months (198)	13
longer ago (172)	8
never (892)	3

Database: current account holders

How Banks and Building Societies Compare

Comparing your bank with your building society which do you think…?

	Building society %	Bank %	No difference %	Don't know %
has the more convenient opening hours	74	7	15	4
offers the quicker counter service	39	25	31	5
has the friendlier staff	32	18	46	4

If building societies were able to offer a range of banking services such as those listed, which, if any, would you like your building society to be able to provide you?

	%
Cheque book facilities	56
Payment of standing orders	39
Cash dispensers	32
Personal loans	28
Travellers' cheques	26
Overdraft facilities	20
None of these	23
Don't know	3

Analysis (base)	Percent replying 'None of these'
All respondents (834)	23
Age: 15-24 (108)	16
25-34 (204)	22
35-44 (190)	22
45-54 (111)	20
55-64 (134)	28
65+ (87)	36
Class: AB (218)	27
C1 (276)	22
C2 (224)	21
DE (116)	23
Usage of bank services: heavy (295)	22
medium (349)	23
light (190)	26

Database: Current account holders at bank and building society

What Services Bank Customers Would Like

(A) Which, if any, of these changes would you like to see your bank introduce and (B) which three or four would you most like to see introduced?

	Most liked introduced (A) %	All liked to be introduced (B) %
Saturday opening	41	51
Longer weekday opening	21	28
Improved system of queuing	21	29
Increase £50 limit on cheque guarantee cards	18	25
More tills open at lunch time	18	27
End charge for cashing other banks' cheques	18	29
Details of how bank charges are calculated	16	25
More cash dispensers outside banks	16	23
More frequent bank statements	14	21
Easier access to your manager	6	11
More information on banking services	4	9
Increase limit on cash dispenser withdrawals	4	7
Easier access to loans or overdrafts	3	5
More cash dispensers inside banks	3	5
Higher limit on credit cards	2	5
Credit cards more readily available	1	2
Longer hours/Saturday opening/ more tills at lunchtime	59	67
None of these	19	11

Database: current account holders

Why Customers Opened a Bank Account   (Note how convenience is a priority even with automated money machines.)

Why did you open an account with (name of bank) and why did you open an account at that particular branch?

Percent of all respondents

Convenience – most convenient for home/work / *only* convenient bank	54
Advertising	26
Employment link – company deals with it/pays wages into it	21
Familiarity – previous dealings/recommendation of family, friends/ work for them	18
Specific services – interest on current accounts/ low or no bank charges/ Saturday opening	15

Database: new current account holders

Should Banks Explain Charges?   A large majority (82%) felt that banks should show calculation of bank charges on each statement containing such charges – only 9% felt that they should not (8% had no opinion on the matter). People held this opinion whether they had paid bank charges in the past twelve months or not.

Do you think banks should show the calculation of bank charges on each bank statement containing such charges?

	%
Yes	82
No	9
Don't know	8

Analysis (base)	Percent replying 'yes'
All (1284)	82
Sex: men (656)	82
women (628)	83
Age: 15-24 (172)	87
25-34 (283)	85
35-44 (276)	85
45-54 (181)	82
55-65 (207)	78
65+ (165)	73
Class: AB (293)	77
C1 (376)	84
C2 (373)	85
DE (242)	80
Usage of banking services: heavy (388)	81
medium (517)	86
light (379)	77
Bank charges paid in last 12 months: yes (567)	85
no (533)	81
Statement received: once a month+ (600)	83
less often (624)	82
Opened first account: in past 6 years (300)	85
over 6-10 years ago (226)	86
over 10 years ago (758)	80

Source: *Banking Services and the Consumer*,
National Consumer Council report,
published by Methuen, 1984.

2 Who Are the Bankers?

7 Britain's First Banks up to the Arrival of the Career Banker

Today's multi-billion-pound international corporations are a far cry from the medieval days, when money-lenders were outcasts and when 'banks' were no more than the despised tradesmen whose personal fortunes were tapped by kings to pay for hopefully profitable wars.

Britain's First Banks

Five hundred years ago banking was a high-risk gamble. The great trading families of Florence who amassed their fortunes by first running, then simply financing, merchant fleets were courted by princes in need of gold for their armies. A lost war, or a royal rebuff to calls for repayment, could mean writing off the loans.

King Edward III, for instance, simply refused to pay the royal family's debts to Florentine bankers Bardi and Peruzzi when he came to the English throne in 1327. Only a suicidal banker would have attempted a stern talk to an absolute monarch about his overdraft, even over the medieval equivalent of a glass of the manager's sherry. So when the King washed his hands of the debts, the banks collapsed.

It was an inauspicious start for formal banking in Britain. But the finance needs of English merchants in their trade to and from the continent ensured a growing queue at the money-lenders' tables, their 'benches', or 'banks'.

By the mid fifteenth century Cosimo de Medici had opened a London branch of his international bank. The Medicis handled deposits and loans from their Florentine headquarters and across Europe from branches in the merchant cities of Avignon and Bruges, as well as in London.

This time it was the spiralling costs of the Wars of the Roses that caused King Edward IV to follow the family tradition of defaulting on his loans. Despite efforts to agree on extended terms for the money, the Medici bank had to write off the royal debts and close its London office.

'Usury', or charging interest on loans, was illegal in England until 1546, so home-grown bankers were no more than backstreet money-lenders, necessary but universally detested, and not infrequently hounded out of town. In time the goldsmiths began to extend their business by holding gold bullion and plate for customers alongside their normal trade in jewellery and precious metal ornaments, and handing out receipts which, in turn, began to be treated as our earliest form of paper money.

In 1679 a Parliamentary Bill recognized the growing popularity of this form of trade: '. . . several people, Goldsmiths and others, by taking and borrowing great sums of money, and lending out the same again for extraordinary hire or profit, have gained and acquired for themselves the reputation and name of bankers . . .' The sideline of the goldsmiths, the unpopular but necessary work of the money-lenders, and the trading finance deals of the merchants had come together to form a trade in its own right.

Banking was a fiercely competitive business even then. Sir Dudley North, a merchant venturer returning to London in 1680 after twenty years abroad, reported his amazement at being followed through the streets of the City by goldsmiths' men, all trying to persuade him to deposit his wealth with their masters.

City merchants had traditionally kept spare cash in the Mint of the Tower of London. But after Charles II's seizure of that hoard, merchants preferred to trust their money to the goldsmiths' vaults. A number of those goldsmith banks survived into this century, for example Martins of Lombard Street (later absorbed by Barclays),

Childs of Temple Bar, and Hoare of Fleet Street. All have been taken over in the last two or three decades.

Loans were made at rates of interest that reflected the risks, plus substantial profits. In the latter years of the seventeenth century interest rates as high as 33 per cent were not uncommon. And while many of these goldsmith bankers did amass great fortunes, bad debts and overlending forced as many others into debtors' prisons.

It was a chaotic, largely unregulated marketplace for money. No individual bank at that time was big enough to finance the really major projects that the Florentine banks had taken in their stride more than a century earlier.

The Bank of England

In 1694, with William of Orange on the English throne and a war against France to finance, Parliament considered the creation of an entirely new type of bank, one financed by many private investors and with capital enough to lend money to the government. This was a revolutionary idea for the England of that time. Continental company banks had been formed in Amsterdam and Genoa, and they operated well. But in England it was not the financial but the political risks that caused an outcry.

As long as Parliament controlled tax-gathering it controlled the royal purse. In that way Parliament could moderate the authority of the King's government. The creation of a bank wealthy enough to finance a war was seen as a serious threat to this hard-won political balance.

There was also a sharp divide on party political grounds over the issue. Tory landowners feared, with some justice, that the bank would be financed by their opposing Whig merchants. Only the merchants had the cash on hand to subscribe to set up the bank, and so they would be able to appoint its directors, and control its policy.

Despite a fearsome Parliamentary battle, the Bank of England was formed, and its £1,200,000 capital was subscribed by wealthy investors within 10 days. The bank agreed to lend money to the government at a flat rate of 8 per cent interest and, in return for its help, the bank was given the right to issue notes which swiftly became recognized as a safe alternative to gold. The bank 'promised to pay the bearer' of its notes in gold on demand.

The bank set up offices in rooms within the textile traders' exchange, the Mercers' Hall on Cheapside in the City, 'furnished with pens, inke, paper and sand'. Its first Governor, Sir John Houblon, was the grandson of a Flemish Protestant Huguenot refugee. He engaged the country's first career bankers, just 17 clerks and 2 door-keepers.

The Bank's Political Rival

Having succeeded in creating one bank, the King's friends in Parliament set out to create another a couple of years later when the royal fortunes were again running low. The Bank of England didn't have sufficient capital to make a second major loan to the government and so the idea of a 'Land Bank' was proposed. This time only Tory supporters would be allowed to put up capital. Salesmen were dispatched to the Shire counties to persuade local Tory squires to invest, and offices were opened to receive the money.

After three weeks only £1,500 had been raised. The second bank idea had been a disaster, and the whole principle of subscription banking had been put at risk.

King William, with an army in Flanders that was expected to desert at any moment if it didn't get its pay, had to send the Duke of Shrewsbury to the directors of the Bank of England with an appeal for an urgent additional loan of at least £200,000. The bank agreed, called on its shareholders, and the extra money was raised. The King got his loan. The war continued. And the bank's key role in the whole affair confirmed its position as an effective part of the country's establishment. It received further privileges in return for the additional loan. It was granted a monopoly as the country's only company (as opposed to private or family) bank.

In 1708 an Act of Parliament underlined this monopoly, confirming that no corporate body or partnership of more than six persons should 'borrow, owe, or take up any sum or sums of money on their bills or notes payable on demand at any time less than six months from the borrowing thereof'. So this law didn't bar commercial lending, but it did make it impossible for anyone other than individuals or families to provide regular short-term loans.

Not that this monopoly put the Bank of England above the financial risks of the marketplace. Just a few years after that Act of Parliament, the bank, together with dozens of the smaller goldsmith and family banks, came close to disaster when the South Sea Bubble burst.

The South Sea company, set up to trade with the Spanish territories of South America, created the country's first stockmarket boom, and its first market crash.

Backed by members of the government and with the King as its Governor, the South Sea company attracted frantic investment buying for a grandiose scheme to take over much of the national debt. Its astonishing success in attracting the savings of rich and poor alike spawned a hundred imitators. Company promoters dazzled investors with schemes to finance vessels to Africa, to drain the Cambridge Fens, to create a 'perpetual motion machine', and even for a system that claimed to be able to extract silver and gold from base metals.

To keep the price of its shares high, the South Sea company pressed its friends in government to outlaw all the companies without a Royal Charter who were advertising for investors. This was done early in 1711, and the value of those companies' shares, along with their dreams of gold mountains and exotic trading ventures, fell away to nothing. To the horror of the South Sea company's directors, their own shares also started to fall in value.

The gambling public lost its nerve. South Sea shares, valued at £900 apiece at the peak of their fortunes, dropped in price by as much as £100 a day. The Bank of England was called in to help, and was persuaded to assist its rival by buying South Sea shares at £400 a time to try to stem the flood of panic selling. But, when the South Sea company's own bankers went bust a few days after that deal, nothing could prevent investors from selling at whatever price they could get. And now the Bank of England itself was drawn into the crisis.

Queues of bank customers lined up at its counters demanding to withdraw their deposits in gold. No one trusted 'paper money' any more, not even the notes issued by the reputable Bank of England.

As the history of the bank records, the crisis was such that the counter clerks were forced to slow down the drain on deposits in any way they could: 'Payments were made in light sixpences and shillings, and large sums were paid to particular friends, who went out with their bags at one door, to deliver them to people placed at another who were let in to pay the money to tellers who took time to count it over. These persons were, of course, always served first. By this means time was gained, the friends of the bank rallied around it, and made large subscriptions to support the company.'

The bank was saved. But when the South Sea Bubble burst, it impoverished peers and commoners alike, caused near riots of recrimination in Parliament, embroiled the King in a scandal, and discredited the whole idea of share dealings for some generations.

The Bank of England's dominant position in the commercial life of London was not challenged again for more than a century. But, from its newly built banking hall in Threadneedle Street in the City, it could not alone serve the financing needs of a country fast emerging from the constraints of a medieval economy.

Home-grown Bankers

Across Britain agricultural reforms created demand for capital to improve land and stock. Money was raised by landowners and businessmen for thousands of miles of privately built turnpike roads, for canals, and for the new factories and mills harnessing water power. Local country banks emerged in market towns to meet the needs of expanding business. There were 300 such private banks by 1780, and over 900 by 1815, all issuing their own paper money.

These provincial banks were family-owned or one-man businesses. Some of the most enduring were set up by Quaker landowning families. The Quakers had forged close bonds of mutual trust during their years of religious persecution. These inter-family links, and their traditions of financial prudence, combined to form an ideal basis for an informal banking network.

In the City of London itself, the heirs to the surviving goldsmiths' banks were able to expand their businesses. So too were the Jewish bankers, many of whom moved to London as Holland's prosperity declined. The Napoleonic Wars speeded this shift of banking expertise from continental cities to the relative peace of London. And it further confirmed the stability of the capital's banks grouped around the Bank of England.

Dashing Merchant Bankers

In 1805 Nathan Rothschild set up his office in London, and soon revealed a style of banking that had not been seen since the great days of the Florentine merchant princes.

Nathan's father, Mayer Amschel Rothschild, sent four of his five sons from the family's bank in Frankfurt to the other financial capitals of Europe – Paris, Vienna, Naples, and to the City of London. The Rothschilds then established an international intelligence network that worked efficiently across the war-torn continent. Couriers, specially chartered sailing ships, carrier pigeons and a discreet army of commercial and political agents amassed and exchanged information that made it possible to gauge banking risks. In a matter of years, the Rothschild family became the most important bankers in Europe and set the pattern for today's international merchant banks.

Britain's domestic banks might take significant risks as they financed purely local developments. But it was the merchant bankers – the Barings, Hambros, Kleinworts and Schroders and the famous Rothschilds – who caught the public imagination as real financial venturers.

Rothschilds financed the development of Russia's oilfields; they financed Cecil Rhodes's gold and diamond mines in South Africa; and, in 1876, they enabled Prime Minister Benjamin Disraeli to buy from the Egyptians a half-share in the new Suez Canal, which saved ships having to sail all the way round the Cape of Good Hope and the huge continent of Africa – a short cut to India and the Far East that saved money as well as time.

Barings, the oldest of London's merchant banks, was described by Louis XVIII's minister, the Duc de Richelieu, as one of the 'six great powers of Europe', alongside Britain, France, Prussia, Russia and Austria. From its London offices Barings helped the United States to buy the lands beyond the Mississippi from France, even though the deal was at the height of the Napoleonic Wars. Barings also financed the building of the US railroads, and very nearly crashed when giant loans to South America went wrong in the 1890s.

Money Capital of the World

These spectacular banking coups were a far cry from the bread-and-butter business of the average, very localized British banker of those times. Even then, however, there was nothing dull about this country's business when Britain emerged victorious from the Napoleonic Wars in 1815. London had become the unrivalled financial capital of the world.

Most City banks were still owned and managed by single wealthy families, following their merchant traditions by dealing in gold and foreign currencies, raising loans for governments and for business schemes across the world. With the British fleet as the most efficient debt collector in the world, and British governments generally willing to send a gunboat or two to transform a commercial argument into an excuse to expand the Empire, these nineteenth-century private bankers had a comfortable life.

Walter Bagehot, writing later in the century about the London banker, noted that the very title had especially a charmed value. 'The calling is hereditary; the credit of the bank descends from father to son; this inherited wealth soon brings inherited refinement. Banking is watchful, but not a laborious trade. A banker, even in large business, can feel pretty sure that all his transactions are sound, and yet have much spare mind. A certain part of his time, and a considerable part of his thoughts, he can readily devote to other pursuits. And as a London banker can also have the most intellectual society in the world if he chooses it, there has probably very rarely ever been so happy a position as that of a London private banker; and never perhaps a happier.'

Over 70 such private banks operated from mansion banking halls around the City in 1815. And although they tended to regard the financing of the country's growing world trade as their primary business, these London banks did provide some services for the hundreds of small provincial banks growing up across Britain. The big banks lent their names and reputations to smaller provincial houses, honouring bank drafts for their customers, and by holding their gold deposits many became the London arm of dozens of smaller rural concerns. The bankers' banks in turn looked to the Bank of England as the top of this commercial pyramid.

Beyond a Family Business

However, it soon became clear that neither London's private family banks nor the small rural banks had the resources to provide the kind of financial backing British business was beginning to need. Between 1797 and 1819, 300 of these local banks failed, and such collapses often had terrible consequences for local farmers and the new breed of manufacturer. If a town's bank failed, it carried with it to the bankruptcy courts those local traders who had come to rely upon its paper money. There seemed no way around this problem as long as the Bank of England retained its monopoly as the only company bank in England.

In Scotland there had been no such limitation on the formation of company banks. The Bank of Scotland was formed in 1695, the Royal Bank of Scotland followed in 1727, and the British Linen Bank, set up initially to act as a financier for Scotland's linen manufacturers, opened its doors in 1746.

In a financial crash in 1825, over 60 country banks in England and Wales and a number of London's more speculative private merchant banks collapsed. The following year Parliament reacted with laws designed to enable businesses to create banks with adequate resources, and to provide the country with a secure paper currency.

The first of these laws allowed investors to pool their money to create 'joint stock', or company banks, 'except in London and within a distance of 65 miles thereof'. That protected the Bank of England's position, but it opened the door for new, bigger banks to serve the rest of the country. The second law enabled the Bank of England to open branches outside London (a freedom it showed little enthusiasm to exploit), and tightened up the rules on the issue of private banks' paper money.

Now that they were allowed to expand beyond a single family's fortune, groups of wealthy landowners and manufacturers came together to form banking companies. The progress towards today's system gathered pace a few years later when the Bank of England's

old monopoly was further challenged by businessmen who formed
'banks of deposit' which used customers' savings as well as shareholders' capital to finance loans.

A formal change in the law in 1833 finally ended the Bank of
England's monopoly as a company, even in London. And in 1834
the London & Westminster Bank was founded, to be followed by
the London Joint Stock Bank two years later, then the Unions, and
County Banks in 1839.

The Career Bankers

All these changes brought with them an entirely new type of career
banker. Although many of the provincial family banks came together
to form these new joint stock companies and preserved the father to
son succession of management, there was also room now for out-
siders – the salaried managers and their staffs.

Not everyone liked the change. Banks run by professional managers and owned by anonymous shareholders didn't appeal to traditional 'landed' customers, who were used to dealing face to face with
proprietors. Loans once arranged on the basis of a customer's good
name alone were now being scrutinized by managers with an imper-
sonal but prime responsibility to shareholders and depositors. Banking began to move on to a professional business footing.

The industrial revolution that began to transform Britain in the
first half of the nineteenth century accelerated the pace of change in
the business. The new joint-stock banks were not yet large enough to
meet the demands of growing business. And when small provincial
banks extended credit well beyond their resources, the mildest
recession could spark another round of collapses. Something had to
be done to ensure that businesses taking calculated risks to expand
didn't also have to gamble every time they accepted payment in one
of the hundreds of different forms of locally issued paper money
then in circulation.

Safe Bank Notes at Last

The 1844 Bank Charter Act made the Bank of England solely repon-
sible for the issue of new notes. Banks already issuing their own

paper money were regulated, but not stopped. In fact, the last private bank in England to issue its own notes, Fox, Fowler and Co., continued to do so until 1921 when it merged with Lloyds Bank. In Scotland banks were and are allowed to continue to produce their own bank notes.

The irresponsible issue of notes by insecure banks was thus stopped and a degree of stability was brought to the business. Banks still collapsed from time to time. But those that survived grew as the British manufacturing economy itself grew. And grow it did, with the rise of the industrial centres of the Midlands and with profits from international trade carried on safely under the protection of Britain's unchallenged naval supremacy.

By 1870 the United Kingdom was responsible for one-third of the total manufacturing production of the world. Britain's bankers celebrated their growing wealth by building their cathedrals of money, the arrogantly confident bank buildings that still stand in many town centres today.

More and more of the old provincial family banks merged with the successful joint-stock companies, or formed their own. The last to make the change was Barclays, an alliance of twenty mainly Quaker family banks which came together in joint-stock form in 1896.

By the beginning of this century the top eleven joint-stock banks handled all but a tiny proportion of the country's domestic banking business. Management, however, remained the preserve of the traditional banking families and their heirs. Although a whole new class of salaried staff filled the clerical and under management posts, a sharp line remained between the 'officers' and 'other ranks' of the business.

8 The Rise of the 'Big Four'

In 1914, at the beginning of the First World War, David Lloyd George wrote that 'Money was a frightened and trembling thing.' He was Chancellor of the Exchequer at the time, and he warned his Cabinet colleagues that banks and industrialists alike 'were aghast at the bare idea of our plunging into the European conflict'.

The bankers' horror of war was understandable. The pound sterling was the world's prime trading currency. British banks, particularly the merchant banks of the City, dominated the international financial stage.

Customers also took fright at the prospect of a conflict that could only disrupt trade and put their savings at risk. They queued up in high street branches throughout Britain demanding to exchange notes for gold sovereigns. First the banks rationed their depleted gold stocks, then they refused to part with them. Indignant customers of the commercial banks made their way to Threadneedle Street, to take the Cashier of the Bank of England at his word and test his promise to 'pay the bearer' in gold. Bank Governor Walter Cunliffe decided to 'meet the situation like lions'. Tellers paid over as many sovereigns as customers demanded and, in a few days, although the Bank's own gold reserves ran dangerously low, the panic passed.

The Bank of England's role increased as the war dragged on. The Governor browbeat the commercial banks' directors into line with government policy of restricting and eventually banning the use of precious foreign currency for any private use. Britons became used to banking with notes alone, as the familiar gold sovereign was withdrawn from circulation.

Farewell to Gold

It was not until 1925 that Britain again tried to back its bank notes with gold in a vain attempt to recapture the stability of the pre-war days. But even then no attempt was made to reintroduce gold into domestic banking. In the wake of the great stock market crashes of 1929 that smashed banks across the United States and Europe, Britain's National Government finally released the Bank of England from its obligation to sell gold at a fixed price. In effect, by 1931 the last link with the longest-standing banking tradition had been severed. There was no longer even the pretence that every bank note in circulation represented a store of gold in some banker's vault. Not that anyone in the Britain of the late 1920s and early 1930s would have been too bothered about the financial niceties of the 'Gold Standard'.

In the depths of the economic depression, many of the country's traditional industries were laying off workers and cutting wages. In 1932 more than 1 in 5 of the working age population was out of a job, and, as those figures exclude women, even that doesn't show the true extent of the slump. Then as now, however, those with employment saw their purchasing power steadily increase.

Prices actually fell in the shops. Houses were cheap to buy, home loans cost just 2 per cent to borrow. A secure job mattered more than a well-paid job, and even the meanest-paid junior clerk in a major bank counted himself lucky to be in a career for life.

City without a Role

The formerly dashing merchant bankers of the City were far less lucky. Their world had been smashed with the opening shots of the First World War. It had not been possible to reassemble that London-dominated world of international finance after the peace. Britain was economically worn out. Its overseas investment had been transformed into massive overseas debts. The Edwardian world of free trading across frontiers had turned into a nightmare of national trade barriers, built in the vain hope of protecting battered local industries. The merchant banks dared not make loans to the few international customers who did turn to the City of London. And Victor, later

Lord, Rothschild reported that working in a City bank in 1931 was 'moribund, boring, rather painful'.

The City was still a place of bankers who looked overseas, albeit rather sadly now, with many a wistful glance back to the happy pre-war days. In the same year that Victor Rothschild complained about the boredom of working life in the former world banking capital, a government report confirmed that City financiers were 'more highly organized to provide capital to foreign countries than to British Industry'.

The City's money merchants did make an effort to substitute some of their lost overseas trade by dabbling in the home market. But the City banks' dull country cousins had by now grown, through amalgamations and by the steady accumulation of deposits, to a size where they comfortably provided all the banking services the few British growth industries needed.

Mergers in the High Street

The high street banks of the 1930s had names still familiar to us now. Mergers had created the 'Big Five' national banks of Barclays, Midland, Lloyds, the Westminster and the National Provincial. They stood apart from the smaller banks – District, Martins, Williams Deacon's, Glyn, Mills & Co., National Bank, and Coutts & Co. – which in turn were far larger than the few remaining small regional banks. In Scotland, the National and Commercial and the Royal stood as the commercial giants alongside the Bank of Scotland.

When in 1928 the Treasury made it plain that it would frown on any further concentration of banking power, the mergers stopped, and the industry scarcely altered its shape for another half century.

The Big Five banks tended not to poach each other's customers, let alone their staff. A Barclays or a National Provincial man expected to remain so for the rest of his working life. High-flying career bankers could make progress towards the dizzy goal of a branch managership by, perhaps, their mid 50s. But the higher reaches of the banks remained as firmly closed to the average employee as ever. As late as the mid 1860s an *Economist* survey showed that one quarter of all the country's bank directors were Old Etonians, exactly the same proportion as in 1935. Even in the 1960s only 9 of the country's 221

bank directors were career bankers as such, either active, or retired
general managers.

Holding on to the Past

Victorian paternalism characterized the banks' approach to their
staff, as well as to their business. It survived through those years of
amalgamations in the 1920s and was, if anything, reinforced during
the years of the depression, when staff were glad of a job at any price.

Another war, and another set of rigid government controls on the
whole of the country's finances, prevented any radical changes in
the banking world of the 1940s. Staff returning from the services in
1945 took over their former jobs, and found that little had changed
in their high street branches.

Paying Back the Bankers

In the City, the end of the war and the election of a Labour government brought the Bank of England to the very top of a long list of
businesses to be nationalized. The state takeover merely legalized
what had already become the Bank's role, as the City's reigning
institution and policeman. But it was dealt with ahead of the far
more important nationalization Acts which brought coal, steel and
the railways into public ownership.

Taking over the Bank of England was an irresistible assertion of
government authority over the whole banking system by ministers
who, as the angry young men of the depression years, had put much
of the blame for the country's economic plight (and incidentally, for
the crisis that led to the collapse of the first Labour administration)
on what they regarded as the short-sighted policies and greed of the
bankers.

In the City mansions of the merchant bankers, butlers still served
vintage claret in panelled dining-rooms. But the City of London had
long lost its position in the international financial world; and business now centred on advising the hunter or the hunted on the takeover battles between British companies, or handling the investment
work of the sleepy, but immensely rich, pension funds. The merchant banks' competition for big business banking at home did, how-

ever, help to spur the high street banks out of their unchanging complacency.

Asleep in Marble Halls

On the principle of lending money only to people rich enough not to need it, the high street banks of the late 1940s and 1950s made few attempts to drum up new loan business. And they didn't push too hard for new deposits either. In the 1950s less than a fifth of working-age people in Britain had a bank account. The average worker put his or her weekly cash wages under the mattress, into a Post Office savings account, or into a building society. Ordinary working people wouldn't have dreamed of entering one of the intimidating-looking bank branches, with their marbled Victorian halls and hushed air of financial reverence.

Counter staff dealt with their customers with a kind of deference that had long disappeared in shops. It could be positively unnerving when, with all due ceremony, a customer was ushered into the presence of a manager. All the banks offered the same rates of interest on deposits; inter-bank competition was considered to be undignified and unnecessary.

Merchant banker Lord Brand summed up the divide between the two sides of the banking business in those post-war years. Comparing the high street and the merchant banks, he said: 'They live on their deposits, we have to live on our wits.'

Saved by the Time Zone

Those City wits were sharp enough to revive London's position as a major international financial market in the late 1950s and 1960s. They did so by developing the international side of their financial services generally, and by becoming a trading centre for 'Euro-dollars'. That's the name for dollars held outside the United States and permanently in transit from bank to bank and from country to country. It's also the shorthand for a complex and gigantic international money market. London's geographic position also enabled its traders to make the most of new telecommunications systems which allowed them to deal by telephone or telex with Tokyo's money markets in the morning, with New York in the afternoon, and with California in the evenings. The City was saved by its expertise, its wits, its strong domestic financial market and, to a great extent, by its time zone.

The high street banks, meanwhile, had begun to wake up to the Britain of the 1950s and 1960s. In 1958 Barclays Bank took a share in one of the country's largest hire purchase companies and led the way for banks into the wider world of household loans. Banks began to publicize personal loans for cars, washing machines and all the other consumer goods being bought by families who, in Prime Minister Harold Macmillan's words, had 'never had it so good'.

From the mid 1950s there was a dramatic expansion in the number of bank branches. After 15 years of war and post-war building restrictions there was an enormous backlog of renovation work as well as a clear need for more branches to serve newly expanding towns.

Even without a conscious drive for new business, demand for personal banking services was growing at the rate of 6.4 per cent a year by the mid 1960s and, although the banks invested heavily in automation, staff numbers continued to rise, from around 100,000 in the early 1950s to 163,000 in 1964.

Of the total administrative, clerical and technical staff in banks at that time, 48 per cent were women. Above them, in the offices of the bank's management, women secretaries were common enough, and the banks' personnel departments appointed the occasional woman officer to deal with that army of female juniors. Otherwise, banking remained man's business.

A stinging attack on the complacency of the banks by the government's Prices and Incomes Board in 1967 showed just how little had really changed inside these cautious and comfortable Victorian companies, despite their new computers and their modern glass and concrete buildings. The report attacked the banks' mutual agreement to maintain common interest rates, a policy which prevented any unseemly competition for customers and which ensured high profits. It attacked banking hours, which remained geared to keeping staff costs low rather than to customer needs. It criticized the banks for overmanning because of the duplication of branch networks. And the report attacked the banks' traditions of extreme secrecy, in publishing selected highlights of their results which gave little clear indication of their real profits.

The 'Big Four'

The same report also revealed that the Bank of England and the Treasury would not oppose another round of bank mergers to cut down on wasteful duplication of branches. Bank boards met and talked, and a series of mergers followed which turned the high street's 'Big Five' into today's 'Big Four'.

The National Bank of Scotland and the Royal Bank of Scotland joined forces. And early in 1968 the Westminster and the National Provincial announced that they were to amalgamate, to create the National Westminster Group. However, talks between Barclays, Lloyds and Martins were regarded as taking the Treasury's hint rather too literally. The Monopolies Commission was called in, and rejected that idea. It argued that 'such competition as there is among the clearing banks is likely to be keener with four large clearing banks than with three banks, with one as large as the other two combined.' Barclays absorbed Martins, but Lloyds remained independent.

The 'clearing' banks (so called because they handle the exchange and settlements of cheques between them through a 'clearing house' system) had now settled into the form we recognize today. Most of the smaller banks now lay within the corporate networks of the industry's new giants. The District Bank, and Coutts & Co., bankers to every royal family since George III, were already owned by the National Provincial, and so merged into the Nat West Group. Glyn Mills and Williams Deacon's had long since become part of the Royal Bank of Scotland, and National Bank had been absorbed into the National Commercial Bank of Scotland. The basic shape of high street banking as we see it today had been settled. But not its role.

That critical report on the banks did cause some soul-searching among their managements. Yet, less than a year after the report's attack on cosy informal agreements that prevented effective competition, just such a gentlemen's agreement was reached over bank opening hours.

To sidestep any major revision of their pay scales the banks unanimously closed for business on Saturdays. 'Chronic staff shortages' were blamed for a decision which ensured that banks were open only when most of their customers were at work. The idea of looking at the problem the other way round, and appointing and paying the staff necessary to keep branches open when personal customers might find them of use, would have been too radical to win support inside businesses that still tended to regard banking as a privilege as much as a service.

Jet-set Bankers

Even so, the banker of the 1960s, or at least the City banker, began to take on a new, more glamorous image. Bright young graduates, slick-suited and carrying the jet-setters' hard black briefcase, could now boast about being bankers. Overnight fortunes were being made in the commercial property market, and even the high street banks were in the game alongside the City's merchant bankers, marrying up finance and architects to turn construction sites into spectacular paper profits.

Asset-stripping financial conglomerates were in fashion. They would turn dull bank deposit money into exciting venture capital for the takeover and merging of sleepy old manufacturing businesses. Once acquired, those businesses could be broken up, sold or reshaped with the stroke of a pen. Financiers, impatient with the sluggish rewards from traditional manufacturing, were bedazzled by the instant profits to be made by selling factories rather than working them. So too were the banks.

The ending of many of the earlier restrictions on credit in 1971 opened the door for an orgy of lending, and for a marked increase in competition between banks. New fringe banks, eager for growth, appeared in the City, and they fought to lend to property developers with, seemingly, the Midas touch.

American banks swarmed to the City to join in the party, to lend and reap the guaranteed profits from ever-rising property values. Britain's stock market soared. Ordinary bank customers accepted ever heavier borrowing commitments. Domestic inflation began to rise, as Prime Minister Edward Heath tried to stimulate the economy with cheaper money.

The End of the Party

By 1974, everything had begun to go wrong at once. The Arab–Israeli war led to the sudden, economy-battering rises in oil prices. The government had allowed the pound to find its own level on the foreign exchange markets, and the Labour Opposition was quick to point out that it had 'floated the pound, but hadn't taught it to swim'. Sterling slumped in value, and interest rates were forced up to protect it.

Property deals no longer made commercial sense, let alone guaranteed profits, when the cost of borrowing soared. An emergency rent freeze put the final nail in property's coffin. The stock market collapsed, and the country ended 1974 with a winter of discontent when a head-on clash with the unions drove Ted Heath from office. The City's fringe banks began to show signs of collapse, and one or two of the overlent major banks looked deeply uncomfortable.

Into this crisis stepped Governor Sir Gordon, later Lord, Richardson of the Bank of England. He swiftly organized an informed and effective lifeboat of banking support for the immediate victims of the crash. Twenty-six of the fringe banks were discreetly rescued, and as Harold Lever (later Lord Lever and then Labour's financial adviser) told MPs: 'Without the boost to confidence which the lifeboat operation gave, some of these rumours [major banks in trouble] would have tended to become self-fulfilling, and would have been translated into fact. If we had a major established bank which had defaulted – however unlikely that was – I do not know where we could have stopped the course of collapse.

By the end of 1974 the stock market was at its lowest point since the retreat from Dunkirk in 1940. Nat West had taken the unprecedented step of stating in public that it was not in difficulties. Banking's brief period as a fashionable pursuit for ambitious young men was over for a time. To be 'something in the City' in 1974 was a rather embarrassing admission.

The seemingly invulnerable financial giants of the banking world had stumbled and all but fallen in the early 1970s. Only the Bank of England's swift action had saved the day, at the price of far tighter controls on bank lending, and new legislation that set rigid standards for finance companies setting themselves up as 'banks'.

The 1979 Banking Act finally brought together all the formal regulations and informal controls on banking into one coherent law. Until then, as Bank of England Governor Richardson said: '. . . many deposit-taking institutions were effectively unsupervised . . . and the public perception of different kinds of deposit-takers was extremely blurred.' Now 'bank' and 'banker' were defined. Banks in future had to be recognized by the Bank of England as businesses providing a range of banking services, and enjoying a high reputation and standing in the financial community. That covered the existing major banks. Otherwise, the Bank of England had to agree to license any company wishing to trade as a bank. This ensured that newcomers, these licensed deposit-takers, would, in future, be up to standard. The Bank's list currently includes 297 recognized banks, and 296 licensed deposit-takers.

The Rise of Service Banking

In the not so distant days when bank directors were able to mull over policy decisions at leisure, the shocks of the banking crisis of the early 1970s might have put a halt to new ventures for years. But technology and new banking services, plus fierce competition from other financial institutions, have enforced their own pace of expansion.

Having made their first tentative steps into new services in the late 1950s with the acquisition of hire purchase companies, the banks began to develop a whole range of extra businesses beyond traditional 'money banking'.

They bought or developed their own insurance broking divisions. They established 'factoring' businesses, to buy companies' outstanding debts for instant cash at rather less than their face values and then organize collection themselves. They added departments that offered company registration services to customers, and expanded their wills and family trustee services. Investment schemes were devised and sold. Leasing businesses grew, to provide a form of hire purchase for company customers to buy anything from a fleet of oil tankers to executive cars. Computer payroll services were offered, and a mass market was developed for credit cards.

The credit card business alone grew at a staggering pace. When

British banks first offered the US Visa credit cards to their customers in the 1970s, only regular business travellers were accustomed to paying their way by plastic. At the beginning of the 1970s there were under 2 million card holders in Britain, and around 18 million card transactions each year. A decade later, with Barclays, the Bank of Scotland, the Trustee Savings Bank and the Co-operative Bank all issuing Visa cards; and Nat West, Lloyds, Midland, Clydesdale, the Royal Bank of Scotland Group and UK branches of the Bank of Ireland issuing Access cards, there are over 20 million card holders and nearly 300 million transactions a year.

Plastic card banking and credit, the child of the computer age, was adopted as much as a means of relieving the pressure of a tidal wave of paper work on branch staff as an additional service. Yet credit cards, and all the plastic card-driven cash withdrawal and deposit machines inside and outside the branches, have helped to create their own demand.

Instead of holding steady, banking staff numbers have continued to rise despite massive investment in new technology. Throughout the 1970s, banking recorded an average of 3 per cent more jobs each year. In the 10 years to 1983, staff numbers in the clearing banks and merchant banks increased by over a third to over 380,000. And although the pace of growth has now slowed to half that of the 1970s, staff numbers continue to rise.

9 The Future

Technology and competition are the twin challenges facing banks and their staff in the 1980s and beyond.

Until now technology has been welcomed by banks and bank employees alike. Computer power has made it possible for the banks to deal with a vastly increased volume of business over the past 20 years, and has enabled them to pass on the benefits of improved productivity and profitability to their staff. In the mid 1960s bank clerks were still carrying out the tedious and exacting task of totting up the figures for nearly 20 million current, savings and deposit accounts by hand. Today there are twice that number of traditional cheque and savings accounts; there are also 20 million credit card accounts, over 26 million cheque guarantee cards in issue, around 10,000 automated teller machines in operation 24 hours a day, and hundreds of additional personal and business services.

If computers hadn't made it possible to automate much of the clerical work, half the working population in the country would have been behind bank counters struggling to keep up with the paperwork.

Although the number of banking staff has doubled in those 20 years, inflation alone would have forced an even greater increase but for those computers, because each of today's bank accounts is used far more frequently than in the 1960s. Then it was still possible to go on a family shopping trip and pay your way with coins and notes. Now even a modest trip to the supermarket means that the cheque book or a credit card tends to get used. It's a fact reflected in the number of individual transactions cleared between the banks. That has increased twice as fast as the rise in the number of accounts, more than doubling in the last 10 years alone, and involves the clearance of 3,500 million items each year.

Inflation and the progressive switch by employers from cash to

cheque-paid wages only partially explain this increased use of bank
accounts. The banks themselves have switched from their earlier
passive role to become aggressive sellers of their services. In 1980
Barclays' Sir Anthony Tuke, a descendant of one of the Quaker families that founded the bank, said: 'The real challenge to us over the
next few years will be our ability to create the necessary banking
systems and facilities to attract, profitably, the 11 million wage and
salary earners who today have no active clearing bank accounts.'

Sir Anthony and his fellow bankers are no longer too concerned
about capturing the few remaining committed cash-only earners.
Opening an account for someone who still likes to be paid in bank
notes and who keeps savings under the mattress is not too profitable
a proposition. Instead, the banks want to win over those people
who have found that they can live well enough in an increasingly
financially sophisticated economy without needing a traditional
bank account at all. While computer power has enabled the banks
to handle more business, the advances in computer technology have
also lowered the cost for competitors to enter the same mass money-
handling market.

The ending of the banks' virtual monopoly on personal and company financial services is most dramatically illustrated by the switch
in savings away from bank deposit accounts and into building societies, national savings, insurance-linked savings, and the growing
number of alternatives to the clearing banks.

Ten years ago, 28 per cent of all personal savings were held in
bank deposits. That's now down to 8 per cent. The building societies
took the lead as the main home for personal savings in the early
1970s, and they have increased that lead ever since, despite the
banks' active entry into the mortgage market. Building society competition has spread beyond the battle for deposits to range across
the whole spectrum of personal financial services from insurance
broking to personal loans for things other than house purchase. This
opens the way for building societies to match cheaply, efficiently,
and with similar, often more modern branch networks, virtually any
service that the clearing banks can offer.

Girobank competes with a full banking service through 22,000 Post
Office branches. And the Trustee Savings Banks, recently floated on
the stock market alongside the traditional banking groups, have long

since outgrown their roots as workers' savings clubs to become
active competitors for personal banking business through 1,650
branches nationally.

Changing City regulations have also substantially increased the
number of insurance companies, overseas financial groups, and
investment houses of all kinds offering savings schemes, credit
cards, and cheque accounts directly to the public. Stores groups
are queueing up to introduce their own credit card facilities which,
although they do generate business for the bank-owned credit
card computer clearing systems, also cut into the banks' branch
trade.

To meet this growing competition, the banks have been changing
their approach to domestic business. They have been making the
sometimes uncomfortable switch from being 'product-led' to 'mar-
keting-led' businesses. This means that instead of setting up a service and waiting for customers to come through the branch doors to
use it, the banks are researching their customers' present and likely
future financial needs, then setting out to create the services that
will meet those needs.

For bank branches that means a radical change, from being out-
posts of the old, closed world of money to being 'shops', geared to
selling financial services.

'Money banking' itself, the cheque-cashing and deposit-taking
that has formed the hard core of branch banking business for generations, looks set to become a purely mechanical, or rather electro-
mechanical process.

Automatic teller machines, the through-the-wall plastic card-
driven cash dispensers, already provide the kind of 24-hour, 7-days-
a-week service that manned branches cannot match. The addition
of cash machines inside branches, deposit-accepting machines,
account-handling machines allowing customers to key in their own
changes to standing orders or make direct account-to-account payments themselves, points the way to a new kind of banking.

All the high street banks are currently reorganizing their branches,
bringing staff out from behind their counters to deal with more than
paying out or taking in cash. Specialist small business branches are
on the way, staffed with experts in business loans and with advisory
teams ready to sort out insurance matters, or to handle any of the

financial aspects of setting up and running a business. Home loan advisers are being moved out among the customers, to compete with the building societies on their own ground. And staff training is beginning to reflect this progressive change from handling money to dealing more directly with customers, as people rather than as part of a queue.

The technology that is making possible this change in branch banking is also beginning to force some radical rethinking within the banks. Like a genie let out of the bottle, there is no way that the banks can now force the stopper back down upon technology, wherever it may lead them. The signs are that it is leading them far from their old branch networks.

Any average home computer linked to the telephone by low-cost modem provides all the equipment needed to manage a bank account, to shop, or to make payments to any other computer-linked account from home. The equipment is already here. The systems to make such home shopping and banking networks a reality have already been tested in a limited way by the Royal Bank of Scotland and the Nottingham Building Society. Widespread use of such systems could transform the nature of much banking work and accelerate the move from behind branch counters to backroom computer management. It could also mean the breakdown of localized banking, which calls for thousands of non-specialist managers.

Electronic Funds Transfer at Point of Sale (EFTPOS) systems also point towards an age of banking without paperwork. The clearing banks are planning to have over a quarter of a million of these checkout till card payment systems in shops by the end of the decade. Sliding a card through the electronic reader allows the price of a purchase to be transferred in an instant from the shopper's bank account to the shop's account. No cheques, no credit card slips, no paperwork of any kind. Just an electronic pulse, and an enormous security headache for banks and account holders alike.

Even the less sophisticated new technology can have a radical effect upon the work of bank staff. The wonders of electronic banking may not empty the branches for some years, and the pressures of the competition may in any case refill those branches with salesmen and women trained to turn advice into new business for any of a thousand different bank services. But the introduction of something as basically simple as 'credit scoring' illustrates the impact of new ideas on old working practices.

Credit scoring is little more than a scorecard of points awarded for different aspects of a customer's lifestyle. A high-earning professional in a stable job, owning his or her own home and without sizeable additional debts, might score way above the number of points necessary to be judged a good lending risk. On the other hand, a recently unemployed labourer with a poor past job record, no assets, and seemingly overwhelming personal debts would, clearly, tend to score poorly on any such system.

Before the arrival of computers, able to number-crunch their way through past lending records and come up with average profiles of customers likely to be sound lending propositions, such credit-scoring systems would have been an impossibility. Each local bank manager had to be trained to carry out such loan assessments on an individual basis, working from customers' records and from face-to-face interviews. Now the bulk of that once critical management function can be dealt with by filling in a simple form and adding up the score. Above some average 'good risk' line, the loan is agreed. Below that line, and the case may be reviewed by a manager or the manager's assistants. But these days the computer-designed score cards carry as much weight as a banker's personal judgement in the overwhelming majority of cases. Branch securities staff may also find their work of obtaining and evaluating personal security for loans becoming a thing of the past as the banks rely more on do-it-yourself loan application and credit averages.

This change from personal 'average' banking clearly makes it possible to handle today's far greater volume of business. But in so doing it has undermined some of the traditional calls on the banking judgement of an entire cross-section of bank staff – the non-specialist branch bankers are fast losing their role.

The simple application of a computer average doesn't stop with personal customers. High up the banks' management hierarchy, in one of the most important single sections of any bank, its corporate lending department, very similar credit-scoring devices have crept in with the hardware and software of corporate, even international, debt analysis.

The big company overdraft arranged on a golf course between

bank chief and industrial chairman is becoming a thing of the past. The game of golf may well be played. But the hard-nosed business of lending will be run through computers that 'score' existing debts against earnings forecasts, setting rates of interest against a weighted risk analysis. No king with a good war in prospect would get on to the shortlists for a loan these days unless the computer predicted that he was odds-on favourite to win, and the bank's money market traders could hedge their bets with a little judicious lending to the other side.

While personal judgement is still called for at policy-making levels, the need for corporate conformity sometimes robs middle management of its initiatives and of the reality of career development programmes, aimed at developing a capacity to act independently and to accept delegated responsibility. The scope for using that independent judgement has narrowed significantly in many of the traditional areas of banking.

Tomorrow's bankers face a curious mix of changing roles and prospects. For the very few high flyers able to break through to the senior management ranks, the last decades of the twentieth century can hardly be other than exhilaratingly demanding. For the ambitious plodders with a horizon in the ranks of middle management, their scope must be limited by an increased willingness among the banks to appoint outside specialists to the key jobs in marketing, in computer systems development, and even in the more obviously mainstream financial areas such as investment, insurance and corporate financing. The banks can no longer afford to rely on 'growing their own talent' in the really critical sectors of their business. The scope for good generalists is narrowing.

Progressive deregulation of the British financial system – culminating in October 1986's 'Big Bang' in the City – has forced the competitive pace in banking. As old distinctions between different sectors of the finance industry have been smashed away, the banks have emerged as the senior partners in financial conglomerates offering every personal and corporate service. Quite what effect this broader role will have on the banker as a distinctive character in the financial world remains to be seen.

As for the mass of bank staff, the juniors and branch assistants, the clerical staff and machine minders of the electronic age, it is a future without a known horizon. An increasing freedom from the tedium of basic money-handling work opens up the prospect of greater customer contact for branch staff, and an increasing specialization in training to provide the kind of personal advice that was once the preserve of the manager. But technical changes and sharpened competition put increasing pressure on banks to curb staff expansion, or to trim staff numbers. There's no guarantee of a job for life in a bank any more.

3 Joining a Bank

10 Getting the Job

In the 1950s banks were so short of staff, and so ignored by job-hunters, that advertising agents were told to stop magnetizing new customers until they had attracted new recruits to serve them. The come-hither advertising that emerged was designed and focused on career opportunities for young men, on their chances of being managers in their early to mid 30s. It is said that one or two directors questioned whether or not such dreams did in fact come true, and asked the embarrassing question of how many managers were actually young enough to warrant such advertising.

A check through most of the banks showed that young men, often identified as able and worthy of promotion by personnel managers, were too frequently languishing in ruts, waiting for seniors to die or retire. Promotion was too often handed out strictly on rota, and talent was being overlooked.

Incited by their own advertising, the bank's top men ordered a kind of purge, and younger men were picked for rapid promotion and earlier executive stardom than was the custom. Some of today's managers recall their unpopularity when, as men barely in their 30s, they were promoted above the 50-year-olds. This resentment was natural enough. However, things gradually sorted themselves out as the growth of banks opened up jobs for so many of their more thrusting staff.

Age is less of a bar to promotion today, though there is still an element of waiting for a senior's desk to become vacant. Also these days there are applicants galore, more than could fill the available jobs despite the expansion of the banks' operations. A head office personnel manager can expect to receive at least 200 applications a day during 'the season', on top of those that go straight to the branches or to area offices. The season is around May or June, at exam time, which is why it is best to apply earlier in the year.

It is possible to go from branch counter to boardroom in a bank. A famous example, pointed at by most banks, is Alex Dibbs, who went from grammar school and Dover College to the Westminster Bank in 1935 and, despite having his career interrupted by a world war, became a manager at the Westminster's Croydon branch at the age of 42. From then on his rise was rapid, and he was on the board at 52. He became chief executive of the National Westminster Bank in 1977 at the age of 59. His innovative and modern thinking, as well as his decisiveness, blended with kindness and understanding, made him a natural leader.

His story is the exception rather than the rule, because there are, after all, only a few jobs right at the top of the major banks. But it is still possible to reach the executive offices after starting with no more than a few O-levels – although A-levels are to be preferred, and these days banks are appointing more graduates, who are groomed for the top jobs even earlier in their careers than Alex Dibbs. Whether graduates will prove themselves any better than those with rather less education – or rather, less time devoted to education – has yet to be shown.

The important qualities are common sense and an ability to learn complex procedures as well as a willingness to keep your nose to what in the early years is often a rather monotonous grindstone.

Any staff who want to get on in banking these days must also be willing and able to do the studying needed to pass the often quite tough Institute of Bankers examinations. So a first job in a bank won't mean an end to academic work. Listening to bankers who have made it to the top or even half-way there, it is clear that they have one thing in common. They would do it again, they are glad they have done it. They have found the job satisfying. It has not always been a challenge, though some could tell of distinct challenges with clients and with colleagues as well as with new avenues of work.

Although new technology and increasingly fierce competition may mean an end to the cradle-to-grave security of a banking career, there remains greater security of tenure than in most businesses these days, unless you really make a mess of it by being lazy, dishonest, drunken, or overdoing any of the deadly sins. Sinners in a small way will get frank and free character readings, and only the major sinners are fired. One of the traditional rewards of banking is the knowledge of having a secure living. But redundancy is becoming a factor big banks are having to accept as a necessity. Only those flexible enough to change along with changing banking markets, technology and services can expect to stay the full course of a career these days. There are, of course, a good many fringe benefits. Cheap mortgages, even cheap loans; share ownership and in recent years bonus schemes; reasonable holidays, though not as good as in many other careers; and a social life laid on if you want to participate – leisure activities at a reasonably low cost. The banks take care of their own. They may not show too much love, and they may be rather sparing with the praise, but they are also sparing with the blame, and the big high street banks at least tend to be comforting and protective towards their staff.

Some of the old staff traditions are dying or dead. It was not all that long ago that you couldn't marry under the age of 25 without your bank manager's permission. You could get a subsidized mortgage, but there was an unwritten law about the kind of house you were expected to buy. If it was going to be better than the homes of those above you in rank, you might find the mortgage offer smaller than you had hoped, and 'top-up' loans from sources outside your bank were frowned upon, as they are even today. The traditions were accepted by those grateful for work, but were for the most part swept away in the days when recruits became hard to court.

Face it. Your first 6 months are going to be difficult – often boring, hard work, and with so much information and knowledge being stuffed into you that you may often wish you'd never been taken on. Indeed, the early routine deadens many an ambition, but the transition thereafter to straight branch banking begins to relieve the monotony. You start to see names on the sheets that you sort, and you begin to feel that there really are human links with the world out there, beyond the account books and the endless clerical procedure.

The ground rules for getting into the business are much the same for all types of bank and banking. Let's start with the broad rules and then move on to detail. You may be a school-leaver with just a few O-levels or with CSE grades; you may be a college leaver with A-levels, or a graduate with a good degree. There is a chance for all of you to get on in banking, but – and it is a firm 'but' – everybody starts at the bottom. Perhaps for some the early training may be accelerated. It depends on the person, but the early days are the same for all.

Your Application

You must make a good impression from the start, with your letters and 'curriculum vitae' (these are the facts of your 'public' life so far, and we shall call them CVs from now on). Clear, logical, well-thought-out applications will help you to clear the first hurdle on your way to a banking career, so take special pains over those first letters.

You should write your letters of application early in the year, before you take your summer exams. Your CV won't contain your exam results, but you can at least say what exams you are going to take and give some idea of those in which you expect to do well. Remember that most school-leavers do not apply until after their exams. They may be lucky, but they have less chance than the early birds because there is so much more competition after the exams. If you write early you may be asked to apply again later on, but on the other hand you may get an interview before that and you may even be offered a vacancy before the exam results are known. Your academic qualifications will give you a good start on the age-related pay scale as long as you earn them while in full-time education. However, it is worth hanging on to the idea that the banks appoint you as an individual, and not simply as a list of school or college achievements or prizes. Exam successes help, but they are certainly not everything. They are, however, proof that you have had a full-time education.

You need to be numerate. That does not mean that your arithmetic has to be in the Einstein class, but you should have a feel, an understanding, for numbers, which can and do paralyse some people. You need personality, to be sufficiently un-shy to talk naturally and to answer questions about yourself in such a way that the interviewer gets an impression of the real person you are, with interests beyond the confines of school and prospective banker. Interviews are chiefly a cross-check of your academic ability, a proof that you are telling all or most of the truth.

Any recommendation to appoint you will be based on personal assessments every bit as much as on your scholastic background and achievements. You may have all the good exam results in the world but, if you lack the ability to get along with people, you're likely to get a firm thumbs-down. You will not only be expected to get along well with customers, you must mix at close quarters with your colleagues and you need to be able to get along with them.

Once you have stopped to think about it for a time and decided that banking is for you, think again. Are you sure you are the right sort of person? You will have to toe a number of disciplinary lines, stand a great deal of routine and repetitive work, be discreet in word as well as honest in deed. This is the time to be frank with and about yourself.

Right, you are sure. You and banking are probably made for each other, as much as one can ever be sure of anything in this life.

Write your letter tidily, in your own handwriting. Make it brief. Do not duplicate data that will be detailed in your CV, such as your career and school history. The CV should be typed. If there is no typist in your family or among your friends, try to afford having it done professionally. It must clearly list your education, any work experience you've ever had, your hobbies and ambitions. Include dates – don't leave gaps that might give the wrong impression about where you have spent the odd year or two. Applications or CVs that skip whole 'stretches' of life, at any age, conjure up alarming possibilities for bank personnel departments.

Here are three CVs. Which one would tempt you, as a boss, to interview the person who had prepared it? Which would make you reject the applicant without further consideration?

All apply to the same sort of young man with similar qualifications, but one leaves out too much and another is illegible, messy. The best one (1) may say a little more than the bank's personnel officer wants, but it tells a lot about that John Smith, even including the fact that he likes to have fun and has a gentle sense of humour (see his marital status, for instance). The scrawled, handwritten CV

```
                    CURRICULUM VITAE                    SPRING 1987


John Derek Smith
12 Acacia Avenue
Some Town
Some County, Postcode


Daytime telephone number 01-333 4321

Evening Telephone number 01-999 8765


Born              2 September 1966

Education         Thornton Primary School, Some Town      1971 to 1977
                  Thornton Comprehensive, Some Town       1977 to 1983
                  Thornton College, Some Town             1983 to 1986

Academic qualifications

          O-Levels  Maths, English Language, English Literature, Biology,
                    Art, Economics, French Language
          A-Levels  English Language (B), Sociology (C)


Work experience

Fruit picking at Henderson's Farm, Thornton, in summer vacations, 1979-83
Assistant on petrol forecourt of Ashton's, Thornton, on Sundays, 1980-83
Kitchen Assistant at local public school weekday evenings, 1983-85 (but
    managed to do my college homework as well)
Insurance selling in summer holiday of 1985


Ambition

To succeed and preferably reach the top in a bank or merchant bank.
I feel suited to that kind of business.


Interests and travel

Music, disco dancing, sound reproduction, hi-fi and video, film-making
if I ever got the chance, drawing and water-colour painting.

Holidays include two six-week working holidays in France and in Spain;
visits to my father working in Lebanon (1982) and in Nigeria (1984).

Rugby (school 1st XV), football (at school and in the local team),
sea-fishing and windsurfing when I get the chance and can afford it.


Marital status

Single for a long time yet.


Available

From June 1986 after taking further A-Level in Art.
```

CURRICULUM VITAE   SPRING 1987

John Smith
12 Acacia Avenue
Some Town
Some County

<u>Born</u>   2 September 1966

O-Levels in Maths, English Language, English Literature,
                  Art, Economics, French
A-Levels in English Language, Sociology

<u>Work experience</u>   Took various weekend and holiday jobs through
                  school and college

<u>Interests</u>   Reading, cinema, drawing, stamp collecting.

JOHN SMITH

14 HEMP STREET,
RUSHTON,
RS4. 7SQ.

AGE.. 17¾.
BORN.... 1967, September 4th.
Schools.. Primary School... 1970 to 1972, Second primary
School 1972 to 1973, Middle School. 1973 to 1978, Secondar
-y School 1978 to 1982. College 1982 to 1985.

Qualifications
3 o-levels: English, French, Physics
2 C.S.E.: Maths, Woodwork
1 A-level: metalwork.

Dear Bank manager,

I am writing to you because my dad told me to
work in a bank, and I would like to work in a bank
because I like dealing with money, like my father. I can
work hard, and enjoy working. I usually go to the
bank with my dad, so I can gain more experience
My parents say that I am very honest, which
in time, and I am good with Sums, and Calculators.
I've have always wanted to work in a bank
Since (this is what my parents tell me) I was only
3 years old, I do hope you seriously consider
me for the Job, as you won't be sorry if you
pick me.

Hobbies
Going to Nightclubs on the local Pub, I also like
to play Pool or football, and in a years time, my
dad has promised to buy a windsurfer, I also like
watching T.V. and Playing on fruit machines.
                    Yours Sincerely
                    John Smith

may look like a joke but they happen. Occasionally, it is true. But they do happen.

Don't be tempted to leave out interests like music or dancing, as the second John Smith did. He wanted to present himself as serious and studious, but that is not entirely believable in a young man unless he's so dull as to be unlikely to have the personality to make a go of it in a bank. So just be honest, and reveal yourself and your interests frankly. Remember that personnel officers try to assess you as a human being, not just as a potential trainee.

Do not worry about an obvious talent for art in the most expansive John Smith's CV. Creative thinkers are wanted in banks, not to draw or paint, but to think like artists at times. Whatever your qualifications, exam results and hobbies, be open about them. You will give yourself the best chance of being selected for a job or an interview if your CV enables its readers to judge you as someone they would really like to meet.

Though you should add your A-level grades (in brackets in CV no. 1), you could risk leaving them out if they are bad. Mind you, you will almost certainly be asked for them eventually, on your application form or at an interview. But if by then you have made a good impression as a person, the grades will probably matter less.

It is never a bad idea to inject just the hint of a personal note – under Ambition, Interests, Hobbies, or Marital Status, for instance. You will sound more real, it will help to bring the CV to life, and it will make you appear more human and not merely a cipher with educational qualifications.

Talking of educational qualifications, it is not enough to give these without also naming the schools and/or colleges at which you studied for them. You should also give details of any work experience you have had. Of course, picking fruit and serving petrol hardly prepare you for banking, but the fact that you have had to deal with people and work under disciplines of that kind will make the banks more likely to want to interview you. Any work is good work. You could add that you were saving for a bike, a motorbike, or a car if it's true. That would show an excellent characteristic for a banker.

Your brief letter and CV should go either to the bank's central personnel manager or to your local branch. Individual banks have different policies on this, and you will find the relevant contact address in the chapter on Choosing Your Bank (page 100).

Bank branches sometimes advertise locally, particularly for juniors and secretaries. Buy the local newspapers or look at the copies in your public library. Details of such vacancies are also sent up to the banks' central office departments, so you may well be attacking on two fronts. Never mind, this will heighten the impression of your determination to get in.

Be prepared to write to several different banks, even if you have a particular favourite of your own. There are always many more applicants than jobs and, if you do want to go into the business, you must be ready to throw away any preconceived ideas you may have. Since all offer very much the same sort of salary, training and other benefits, just apply, apply, apply to them all. Add the foreign and international banks to your list – they offer the same sort of career as British banks and for similar pay.

Say where you would like to work, if at all possible. After all, you may need to live at home to start with. As time goes on, however, you must be willing to move with the job. Bank training schemes for anyone interested in progressing beyond purely clerical work involve moves from branch to branch, wherever the promotions may be. During training you will be housed, occasionally rather elegantly in country manor houses that have been bought as training centres. But those conditions apply to later training. In the early months you will be working in the back rooms of the branch that takes you on, and, if you're not in your home town, you may be lodging in a bed-and-breakfast guest house. All the banks have accommodation sections to help find suitable 'digs' if you are away from home.

You will almost certainly be asked at your first interview about your willingness to move. Be honest. It really is no good saying you will move just because you want a job if, when the time comes, you suddenly need to own up to a crippled mother or a premature marriage or some such thing that ties you down. It's unlikely, but it can happen. Be open-minded if you can, but never deceive yourself or your employer.

Read as much as you can about banks and banking. For one thing, it will help to crystallize in your mind how you really feel about the business, whether you are genuinely interested or whether you just want a safe job. We have included a great deal of history and background in this book because it really is important for would-be bankers to know what banking is; that it is as much about people as finance.

Being a mathematical genius is no short cut to being a banker. Being interested, being good at the routine and the disciplines, are good assets. Accuracy is always more important than speed in your basic mathematics, and tends to be regarded as a good quality for potential bank trainees.

Also, when you have read more of the background about banks and banking and have clearer ideas of why you want this kind of career, it makes your conversation at an interview much easier, more natural and undoubtedly more interesting. You will relax more and talk better (though not too much, please). Again it is worth stressing that you should not be afraid to be honest. If your main object is a safe, secure job, admit it, but do not say it is the *only* reason. Don't overplay it. There is no shame at all in wanting safety and security, but let it be part of a rounder, wider, more general approach.

Always try to be and to sound interested and interesting at interviews. Most parents, careers teachers and even people who interview you will breathe a sigh of relief that you want a job as sound as banking, so you have them all on your side when you go job-hunting. You won't have long arguments, as you might if you wanted to be a pop star or a missionary. (But, if you've set your heart on either of those, have a go.)

It is said that the most apparently natural actors, pop stars and singers have rehearsed the part thoroughly. The same sort of thing will apply to you, your letters, your interviews, if you research your subject beforehand. We recommend that you read up a fair amount about banking, and about individual banks, even before writing the first letter of application. Then write what you feel, rather than the kind of thing you imagine a personnel manager wants to read. If you try the latter, you will sound stilted, unnatural.

Walk round your local bank branches and collect as much literature as you can about their various services as well as about the banks themselves. The Banking Information Service (Careers Section) will send you interesting and useful leaflets. The address is: 10 Lombard

Street, London EC3V 9 AT. Besides leaflets on normal banking they have some on secretarial, computer and other specialist jobs.

Once you have written your letter, in your own words and hand-writing, there is no harm in getting a second opinion on it. A careers teacher might be a good editor for you, but do not allow your own personality to be buried or cloaked. A relative might help, but on the whole relatives are biased (either for or against you). Parents are not usually the best advisers and letter-editors because they tend to see everything only from your point of view. They will be so anxious for you to get the job that they may want you to overload the letter with too much detail. Put yourself in the manager's place. He gets so many letters, he wants clarity and brevity, so stick to the essentials.

Whatever you do, make sure you spell correctly and get the gram-mar right – here's where the careers teacher could be helpful. Write, rewrite and then again rewrite the letter until you feel it is just right, then use it for every application, varying only the name of the bank where necessary. We cannot stress often enough that you should never lie – you will almost certainly be found out later. Better to admit to an E grade (at interview if you've left it out of the CV, which is forgiveable) than to lie. Banks follow up references very thoroughly and will have an instinct for details that don't ring true, so they will probably cross-check anything of that kind.

Get yourself a wallet or box file and keep copies of all your appli-cations or, at least, a list of all the people to whom you have applied. Any local instant-print or photostatting shop makes decent copies, and you should keep spares of your CV so that you can dash off answers to advertisements that catch your eye.

Finally, remember to date your letter. Obvious, isn't it? Yet you would be amazed how often letters are sent undated and how such an apparently minor omission can irritate and be noted to your dis-advantage.

Of course it doesn't end there. You will be sent an application form, which will consist of printed sheets asking for even more detail and, at this stage, for personal references. The ideal referee is a former employer, even if you have worked only in the evenings or the holidays. A headmaster, teacher or lecturer can also be helpful (as long as you are sure they won't say terrible things about you). Any adult who knows you reasonably well will do, but no close relatives – no uncles, aunts, cousins. They are regarded as being biased in your favour.

Go to your photostat shop again and get several copies of the application form. Practise filling it out so that your words stay within the lines and the squares. You'll probably be asked to complete the form in your own handwriting, which is less easy than getting it typed because writing takes up more space. Check your spelling and answers. Then, when you are totally satisfied, copy your final draft on to the actual form sent to you by the bank. Use a plain black or blue ink pen, no lurid colours. Banks want individuals, but they are not looking for eccentrics.

Never fail to answer a question – if there is no answer at all, the answer is instantly suspect. If asked for 'languages' and you have none, enter 'None'. You could add that you hope to learn one at evening classes when settled in a job (but only if that's true). Make a final photostat and study it well before the interview.

Nearly all banking interviews are based on the system of pre-selection, which involves accepting and rejecting likely candidates purely on the basis of their letters and application forms. This is why it is so important to get them as neat, readable, comprehensive and presentable as you can. If you get no interview, you get no job.

Winning the Interview

If you are called for an interview, prepare for it in advance. Dress well, not in the height of fashion like Princess Diana or whoever you may consider her male equivalent, but well. Modern as you like but not exaggeratedly so. As always, be yourself. Wear a suit with a collar-and-tie shirt if you have them, but failing that, wear the neatest jacket and trousers you can muster. Ladies should wear a dress or suit, not a top and trousers. Your first impression counts, whoever you visit and for whatever reason. One personnel officer told us about a young man who turned up in jeans for an interview. She had been terribly impressed with the person who showed through his application paperwork, so she started the interview and her impressions were enhanced. She felt he had something but, because of the jeans, she couldn't feel that he was taking the interview seriously. Without mentioning his clothes she made an excuse to call the interview to a halt, and she suggested that he should come back after thinking about why she might have cut him short and why she was asking him to call again.

He more than confirmed her early impression when he came to the second interview in a tidy jacket and trousers, then proceeded to explain why he had worn jeans – he was broke at the time and also rather trying to assert himself as a free soul. She liked his frank admissions, his ability to come to terms, and his latent intelligence. 'Mind you,' she told us, 'he might never have got past the polite good morning if he hadn't revealed so much of himself in his CV and application form. Furthermore, he did have, even on a few minutes' acquaintance, a sort of charisma.' She is proud of her protégé, who became one of the bank's youngest managers at the age of 36 before going into corporate finance departments.

You are not expected necessarily to be able to afford good clothes, but you can always be clean, neat and conventional in your dress. It really is you the bank want to see, not an eyecatching mix of jaunty clothes and gaudy colours. The interviewer will instinctively picture you behind a bank counter, smiling at customers. Being clean is terribly important – clean fingernails, clean hair, clean clothes.

Be punctual. Allow plenty of time for late transport or other hazards. Make sure you know exactly where the interview is to be held. Study your street maps beforehand, but you needn't take them all with you. If it makes you feel happier, get a photostat of the immediate vicinity of your destination. If you don't know which are the nearest buses, stations or tubes, ring up the bank in advance and ask the person on the switchboard. If that doesn't help, get through to the secretary of the person you are going to see and ask him/her. Check on how long it takes to walk from the nearest public transport stop. If it happens to be wet and windy, leave time to tidy up on arrival. Just ask whoever is on the reception desk to direct you to the cloakroom. Freshen up, then go back to be announced. You will feel better if you like the way you look.

We've already warned you to memorize what is on your application form and CV, so that you don't contradict yourself. It's not a bad idea before the interview to put yourself in the other person's place. Try to imagine some of the questions you would ask, then list them and think out your answers. Don't learn the answers off by heart or you will be floored when you are asked something unexpected or unfamiliar. Just be ready with what you think they want to know and you will be much more relaxed.

Don't resent anything that sounds intrusive, too curious about you and your private life. If the questions get to that stage, the interviewer is probably interested in you – if you are going to be rejected he or she will have trouble spinning out the interview to a decent length of time, and you will feel that happening.

The interviewer may want to know what subjects you enjoyed at school and why – these will not necessarily be the subjects you took in your exams. What did you dislike and why? Why choose banking? How far do you hope to get? What will you do if you fail to get into banking? That kind of question is common.

You will also be asked why you chose this particular bank. Hopefully you will have read their literature and have formed some ideas from their advertising so that you can answer well. Don't say something like 'Because you're the listening bank.' All that shows is that you can read, hear, see and remember advertising slogans. Much more to the point is an answer like 'My parents bank with you and so do I.' Or 'I'm afraid I really just want to get into banking and I'm here because you gave me an interview. Since then, I've wanted to go into your bank.' They will know that you must have tried all or most of the banks and will think no less of you for that.

You may be asked what sector of banking appeals to you most. You should have some ideas, and perhaps you will have after reading a little about merchant banks and international banking later in the book. If you really have none, be honest and say that you hope to discover that once you've started work and begun training. If you have some idea – be it contact with customers/computers/handling transactions behind the scenes/clearing/anything, then say so. Say what you think you might most enjoy, though obviously you must express willingness to change your mind as you learn more about the work.

Have some fairly clear idea of your ambitions. These might be anything – you might want to be the bank's chief executive, its advertising genius, its marketing man, a creator of its financial products and packages. You might want to be a branch manager with a preponderance of either personal or business customers. Say something –

anything is better than 'I don't know.' Always make the proviso that you expect to have a clearer view after training.

The interviewer is likely to ask about what you do at home, at play and at games; what your social life is, and what activities you prefer out of working hours. Again, don't be afraid to say music, disco or painting. Of course, it might be good tactics to put something like reading before tennis or the cinema, but for goodness' sake make it credible. Mention three or four leisure pursuits, on the basis that someone leading a full life is more progressive than someone doing little or nothing.

It cannot be said too often that you must tell the truth. Add mountain climbing to your list of pursuits just to endow yourself with bezazz and you could come a cropper. We are prepared to bet our bottom dollar that in such a case your interviewer will turn out to have just spent a sabbatical scaling the Matterhorn, and will launch enthusiastically into detailed conversations about mountain climbing, its pros and cons, the equipment needed and everything you suddenly find you know nothing about.

Eventually will come your turn. All too often, when the interviewer hands the questioning back to the interviewee, there is blank silence. Or, perhaps worse, the only questions asked are about holidays, time off, fringe benefits, that sort of thing. Of course those things count, and you are expected to want to know something about the conditions of employment. But don't put those things first when you get the chance to ask questions.

Try asking what training courses there are, when they are available, how one qualifies for them. Ask about the Institute of Bankers exams – are they advisable, necessary, essential, difficult, manageable? Is there much boring work before you get to the interesting stages? Then ask about holidays, cheap loans, bonuses and benefits, even your pension (looks as if you mean to stay with them). It is never wrong to bring these things up, only to give the impression that they constitute your main priority. You should be seen to be interested in the work rather than the rewards.

All the preparation will be worth while. You cannot paint a room if the walls beneath are rough and uneven. Be ready for that interview and plan the strategy with care. Then and only then will you be naturally unflustered, confident without being over-confident.

You will be a pleasure to be with and neither you nor the interviewer will start wondering how quickly you can escape this ordeal.

You must do all this planning and work because you will be one of thousands, and applicants outnumber vacancies by a wide margin. The more organized and calm you seem to be, the better your chances. The bank's representative is, after all, looking upon you as a potential ambassador to the public, someone whose face, voice and manners must fit.

The same guidelines can be applied to going after whatever job you want. There is never any perfect formula for getting a job, winning an interview, or even making your way on to the short list – luck plays its part. So does the quality – and quantity – of the competition for an ever-varying number of banking opportunities. All you can ever really do is shorten the odds. Riding a short odds horse gives the right attitude – the spirit to win and do it in style.

11 *Choosing Your Bank*

Bank of Credit and Commerce International SA

Staff: UK Banking 2,140 (expanding to 4,000-plus by 1990).
Branches: 45 in Britain; over 360 branches in 68 countries.

The Bank of Credit and Commerce International is a 'licensed deposit taker', a new international bank founded in 1972 with offices in Abu Dhabi, Luxembourg and London.

School-leavers. BCC recruits around 200 school-leavers a year, although the numbers are rising as the bank expands. Minimum entry requirements are 4 O-levels, including English language and mathematics.

Clerical staff are not graded on the traditional clearing bank system because 'we feel that this is restrictive'. Instead, work in branches is shared around, so that staff 'can carry out efficiently any job they might be asked to undertake'. Promotion is on ability, with less than the usual banking emphasis on length of service. Clerical staff may be considered for promotion to supervisory jobs within 4–5 years, and may be promoted to 'officer' status after another 3 years. BCC has its own training college in London. Starting salaries are from £4,800 a year, with benefits including a contributory pension scheme (5 per cent of salary), subsidized loan schemes, private medical health care and luncheon vouchers.

For further information and application form contact:

> The Personnel Officer
> Bank of Credit and Commerce International SA
> 100 Leadenhall Street
> London EC3A 3AD

Graduates.   BCC recruits around 25 graduates each year from all disciplines. Minimum grade 2.2. A 2-year graduate trainee programme combines practical training within BCC branches with academic work. Study facilities for Institute of Bankers – qualifications are available in BCC's training academy in the evenings. 'Progress will depend upon your ability and performance rather than the length of time spent on the job.'

Although an international financial group, BCC's UK staff are more likely to travel abroad than be based abroad. 'Our policy tends to be to employ nationals of the country where we are situated. However, opportunities do occur from time to time in those parts of the world where local employment law allows.'

Salaries 'equate well with others in the banking industry' and are appraised annually.

For further information or an application form contact:

> The Personnel Officer
> Graduate Recruitment
> Bank of Credit and Commerce International SA
> 100 Leadenhall Street
> London EC3A 3AD

The Bank of England

Staff: UK Banking 5,260
Branches: 8

The Bank of England, founded in 1694, is Britain's central bank. It is the government's agent and adviser within the City of London, and the principal supervisory authority of the financial community. It is also the 'banks' bank', holding the accounts of major money market institutions and determining the level of interest rates nationally by setting its own rates as a standard for the other banks. The bank is the sole note-issuing authority for the UK as a whole. It manages government borrowing with the City, holds the nation's gold reserves and, although nationalized since 1946, it is not a government department.

School-leavers.   The Bank of England appoints between 50 and 55 school-leavers with good CSE and O-level GCE results each year, plus another 20 or so A-level entrants.

CSE and O-level recruits normally join the bank's clerical staff, to deal with the mass of paperwork involved in keeping track of the nation's banking system, updating the registers of Government Stock holders or working on the clerical side of the bank's printing operations. Its presses, in Loughton, Essex, design and print bank notes, destroy old notes and produce other documents such as Treasury Bills.

Most staff work in the bank's City of London offices and, unlike the high street banks, customer contact tends to be rare since the overwhelming majority of the bank's 'customers' are other institutions.

The bank looks for young people with a broad general education, whose examination subjects include both mathematics and English language.

A-level recruits must also have enough O-levels to 'prove a sound general education', plus English and mathematics, and must have completed at least 2 academic A-levels. Applications should be made in January before sitting the examinations. If selected for interview, candidates are expected to be able to justify their decision to apply for a job in this unique central institution of the banking system.

Staff have salaries comparable to those of the high street banks. Starting salaries for the youngest school-leavers are around £4,000 a year plus £1,408 London weighting, or around £4,800 plus the London allowance for a new entrant from the sixth form. All staff are on probation for between 6 and 18 months. Holidays range up from 20 days a year plus public holidays, and some departments operate flexitime to enable staff to beat the worst of the rush hour. Fringe benefits compare with the high street banks, and include non-contributory pension, low-cost mortgage finance for staff over 21, loan schemes for season tickets, subsidized dining facilities, and a comprehensive range of social facilities including the bank's sizeable sports club at Roehampton, London.

Applicants are normally required to be British by birth and of British parentage, because of the bank's need to be satisfied that staff fit the requirement to be 'employed as public servants on confidential work'. This rule applies to school-leavers and graduates alike.

Promotion prospects for banking staff are determined by their success in internal training programmes and in the Business Education Council's Higher National Certificate in Business Studies. CSE and O-level entrants normally remain in clerical work within the bank throughout their careers. A-level entrants have opportunities of promotion to more senior management roles, similar to those of graduates. 'The great majority of A-level entrants who stay with the bank can hope to achieve administrative rank', which is the equivalent of middle and upper management in the high street banks.

Application forms and further details from:

> The Principal (Recruiting)
> Bank of England
> Threadneedle Street
> London EC2R 8AH

Graduates.   Around 15 graduates join the Bank of England each year: '. . . we seek not merely those who expect to get good honours degrees, but those who in addition exhibit qualities of maturity, a lively-minded approach to current affairs and a range of interests in which they have played active, and if possible organizational or administrative, roles.' There are no fixed degree subject requirements.

Initial job training is supplemented by a 1-year study course towards the Certificate in Banking for Graduates, at the City of London Polytechnic. Staff who prove likely to be able to progress to upper middle and senior management roles within the bank will find that their initial years involve a changing range of jobs in different parts of the bank's organization. Some staff may be seconded for additional experience in government departments or other institutions in Britain and abroad. The bank expects its graduate entrants to reach junior management levels by their mid to late 20s, middle management in their 30s, and high flyers to move beyond that into the most senior positions in the bank later in their careers.

Specialist Careers for Graduates.   The bank appoints a number of economics graduates, mathematicians, accountants, operational research and data-processing specialists at various times. Data-processing staff normally remain in this side of the bank's operations throughout their career.

For further information contact:

> The Recruitment Manager
> Staff Office
> Bank of England
> Threadneedle Street
> London EC2R 8AH

The Bank of Scotland

*Staff:*9,500
*Branches:*551

The Bank of Scotland was founded in 1695, just a year after the Bank of England. Traditions have not, however, stood in the way of the enthusiastic adoption of new technology or services. The bank was the first to adopt electronic accounting in the late 1950s, and first into the field of home banking in the 1980s. It has been one of the more innovative banks in financing North Sea oil and gas exploration and production, a development that has benefited its international and corporate banking reputation. Its merchant banking subsidiary, British Linen Bank, and its HP and leasing subsidiary, North West Securities, supplement a personal and corporate service through a branch network across Scotland and in major English cities. Personal finance services include the Visa based Bank of Scotland Card. Internationally, the bank has offices in Moscow, Hong Kong and North America.

School-leavers.   The Bank of Scotland recruits up to 1,000 school-leavers annually, although the establishment of its own credit card processing centre significantly increased the number of new staff required in 1986.

Around 400 entrants are taken with SCE Higher grade or O-level passes, and a further 600 with a specific minimum of 3 or more Highers. There are no 'hard and fast' minimum educational qualifications, but non-secretarial staff wanting to have a developing career within the bank need to be able to meet the minimum entry qualifications for the Institute of Bankers in Scotland examinations (3 Highers and 2 O-levels including English, or 4 Highers including English).

School-leavers can, to a great extent, set their own career horizons. The bank encourages its staff to find their own level, and there are ample opportunities to combine in-bank training with more academic study for Institute examinations. Salaries are comparable with those of the other high street banks, plus fringe benefits including free banking, profit-sharing scheme, low-cost personal and home loans, non-contributory pension scheme, low-cost insurance, and a mass of out-of-hours social activities (the bank's subsidized Sports and Social Association alone embraces over 60 clubs).

Staff interviews may be at a local branch or an area staff office, and interviews extend to aptitude tests plus checks of references and school reports.

For an application form write to:

> The Staff Controller
> Bank of Scotland
> PO Box No. 133
> 62 George Street
> Edinburgh EH2 2RA

Graduates. Around 15 graduate trainees are selected each year, and while the bank says that 'given one vacancy and two applicants we might prefer the economics graduate to the graduate in art history', there is no rigid degree preference.

After a 1-year period of basic branch clerical work ('you are not simply going through the mill for appearances' sake; you are learning to respect the mill'), graduate trainees are seconded on short attachments to a wide range of bank departments. This on-the-job experience is paralleled by evening class work, day release study and courses at the bank's staff training centre in Edinburgh to speed progress through the Institute of Bankers examinations. The objective of the programme is 'to equip graduate entrants with the skills and knowledge required to undertake a management position at the earliest possible date'.

Career progress for the most successful entrants would mean completion of training and examination work by the fourth year after entry (moving from Grade 3 to 4 after Diploma examinations are passed, Grade 5 on completion of the initial training period and completion of Associateship examinations), on to branch accountant or equivalent, assistant manager by the early 30s, and management of a smaller branch by the mid 30s.

The Bank of Scotland's chief executive was appointed to the job at the age of 41. That's an exception to the rule, but an indication of the possibilities.

Recruitment is by pre-selection of applications and by interviews, primarily during the 'milk round' university visits of the spring term. The Bank of Scotland's interviewers visit all the Scottish universities and a number of English ones.

Application forms and further details from:

> The Manager
> Training and Management Development
> The Bank of Scotland
> 58–62 St Alban's Road
> Edinburgh EH9 2LX

Barclays Bank PLC

Staff: UK Banking 69,100; UK Group 79,500. More than 100,000 staff worldwide.
Branches: 2,874 in Britain; a further 2,200 branches in 80 countries worldwide.

Barclays is one of the world's largest banking groups. The group includes the Barclaycard credit card business; Barclays de Zoete Wedd (BZW); Mercantile Credit hire purchase and leasing; insurance, investment and international divisions. Merchant banking and stockbroking subsidiaries recruit staff independently.

School-leavers. Barclays recruit around 4,000 school-leavers every year. Minimum entry requirements are 4 GCE O-level/SCE O grade or CSE I passes, including English and mathematics. There are secretarial posts for less academic school-leavers. These may be advertised locally.

Junior banking staff are encouraged to study for the Institute of Bankers examinations and can, in theory, and on past experience, progress from clerical to appointed grades, and on to management and even executive levels of the bank.

Starting salaries range from around £4,000 a year, plus significant supplements for travelling to, and working in, major cities. Permanent staff qualify for free banking, subsidized home loans, specially low staff loan rates, non-contributory pensions, annual salary reviews and work appraisals, plus a 2½ per cent annual cash bonus based on salary.

Clerical staff work a standard 35-hour week, 9 to 5, Monday to Friday. Saturday morning working is paid at overtime rates, with time off in lieu.

For further information or an application form contact:

> Barclays Bank PLC
> Personnel Department
> PO Box 256
> Fleetway House
> 25 Farringdon Street
> London EC4A 4LP

Graduates. Barclay's domestic and international divisions recruit around 55 graduates from all disciplines, and a further 20–30 specifically qualified graduates for specialist departments each year.

As the bank says: 'In selecting graduates, we angle, we do not trawl. We look for a calculated number to supply the future top management needs of one of the largest banking groups in the world. A massive intake of average graduates is not for us. Please do not apply unless you are prepared to endure and enjoy the pressures of getting to the top . . .'

Interviews and selection of graduates normally take place between January and March. The bank's interviewers visit universities, meet-

ing candidates pre-selected from those who have completed application forms.

Graduates join Barclays' management development programme,
which involves completion of the Institute of Bankers examination
to Associate level in 2–4 years, alongside a crash course in practical
banking experience.

Career Prospects.   From junior to middle managment by the late
20s; more senior management by the mid to late 30s. Salaries range
from a graduate starting level of £7,200 (£8,920 in London) to junior
management scales up to around £16,500; middle management to
around £22,500; senior management from £26,500.

For domestic and international division graduate applicants,
further information can be obtained from:

> The Manager
> Graduate Recruitment
> Barclays Bank PLC
> Staff Department
> Fleetway House
> 25 Farringdon Street
> London EC4A 4LP

Specialist Careers for Graduates.   Barclays' computer operations
have grown at such a pace that graduates with computer science or
mathematics degrees have been in particular demand recently. A
normal intake of around 15 graduates with computer aptitude
expanded to 40 in 1985.

For further information contact:

> The Manager
> Central Management Services Department
> Barclays Bank PLC
> Radbroke Hall
> Knutsford
> Cheshire WA16 9EU

Other specialist graduate appointments include an average of 2 economists a year; 2 mathematics, statistics or operations research gradu-

ates for the bank's business research section; and 2 economists for
the bank's Treasury Office. Law graduates (around 2 a year) are
recruited by the bank's trust businesses, and a similar number of
economists or mathematicians are required for Barclays' investment
management teams and at Barclays Unicorn Unit Trust. Further
details from the Graduate Recruitment Manager (see address
above).

Clydesdale Bank

*Staff:*7,000
*Branches:*370

Conventional Scottish branch banking forms the basis of Clydesdale's business. Its branches are concentrated in the industrial west
of Scotland. It offers a full range of personal and business banking
services and Access credit cards. Its 'Counterplus' petrol station card
payment network was one of the first point-of-sale electronic funds
transfer systems in operation in Britain.

School-leavers. Clydesdale recruits around 300 school-leavers
each year from fourth, fifth and sixth forms. Career progress beyond
counter clerical work or secretarial work calls for professional qualifications by examination of the Institute of Bankers in Scotland.
Minimum academic qualifications for the Institute courses are a
Scottish Certificate of Education with 4 passes at Higher grade,
including English, or 3 Highers including English, plus 2 Ordinary
grade passes grades A, B, or C. Older school-leavers with 3 passes at
GCE A-level, or two As plus two Os (including English at A-level
in each case), can start on a higher salary grade.

The most junior new entrants receive starting salaries from around
£3,100. Staff benefits include free banking, non-contributory pensions, housing and personal loans at subsidized rates, a profit-
sharing scheme and a Christmas bonus.

For further information contact your local Clydesdale branch
manager or write to:

The Staff Manager
Staff Department
Clydesdale Bank, PLC
PO Box 43
150 Buchanan Street
Glasgow G1 2HL

Graduates.   Clydesdale has appointed between 5 and 10 graduates annually in recent years, and it operates a special grade scheme of management training similar to that of the Midland Bank. Further information and details from the Staff Manager (as above).

Co-operative Bank

Staff: UK Banking 3,822
Branches: 79, plus some 4,100 in-store 'Handy-banks'

The Co-operative Bank began in 1844 at the curious address of Toad Lane in Rochdale, Lancashire. It had 28 co-operators, and their turnover in the first year was £700.

It was the nucleus of what became the Wholesale Co-operative Society, operating manufacturing, wholesale and finally, on a regional basis, retailing. There are banking counters in the larger Co-op stores.

Opportunities? As good as in any other bank, and this bank is a member of the clearing house in its own right.

Entrants need to have 4 O-levels. Salaries are similar to the 'Big Four'.

Further information from your nearest Co-operative Bank branch – see the Yellow Pages of the local telephone directory.

Coutts & Co.

Staff: 1,800
Branches: 18, mainly in Central London

Coutts & Co. is the smallest of the London clearing banks, and one of the most prestigious. Founded in 1692, and banker to every British monarch since George III, Coutts & Co. is now a 100 per cent owned subsidiary of the Nat West Group. However, it retains its distinct identity and independent management.

School-leavers.   Coutts & Co. recruited 150 new staff in 1985, but this reflects a recent period of particularly rapid expansion of staff numbers. The recruitment total is unlikely to rise substantially in the immediate future.

The minimum qualifications for banking staff are 5 O-levels, grade C or above, including English language and mathematics. High grade passes in CSE examinations are also considered. Ages 16–22.

Starting salaries range from just over £4,000 (excluding a £1,725 London allowance), and staff are eligible for normal banking benefits: non-contributory pensions, subsidized home loans, luncheon facilities or luncheon vouchers, plus participations in the Nat West 2½ per cent annual bonus, and in share option schemes. Staff work a standard 35-hour week, Monday to Friday.

Graduates.   Coutts & Co. recruit 'a limited number of high-calibre graduates with the potential to reach senior positions'. The bank looks for 'all-rounders' rather than specialists to undergo its accelerated training programme. Applicants should be under 25 to train for one of the 300 management jobs in a bank which, although it was one of the first to computerize its operations, still requires some of its gentlemen staff to wear frock coats.

Starting salaries are comparable with the Nat West Group as a whole, and graduate trainees are eligible for the £1,725 London allowance, falling to £420 at the Eton branch and £300 in Bristol.

For further information or application forms contact:

> The Personnel Manager
> Coutts & Co.
> 440 The Strand
> London WC2R 0QS

Lloyds Bank PLC

Staff: UK Banking 47,200; UK Group 54,163. More than 70,000 staff worldwide.
Branches: 2,229 in Britain; a further 500 branches in 48 countries around the world.

Lloyds Bank is the smallest of the 'Big Four' high street clearing banks, yet it ranks among the top 30 banks in the world and has a substantial international business, both directly, and through its subsidiary banks in California and New Zealand. The Lloyds Group includes insurance services, estate agency, a one-third share in the Access credit card operation, leasing companies and stockbroking subsidiaries. More recently, Lloyds has diversified into the Black Horse estate agencies, mortgage business, etc.

School-leavers.   Lloyds recruits around 3,000 school-leavers each year. Minimum entry qualifications for banking staff are 4 GCE O-levels or their equivalent – the minimum to enter the Institute of Bankers Diploma examinations, which specifies English language and one numerical subject, such as mathematics. School-leavers with 2 good A-level passes, BTEC National Certificate, a diploma in business studies or its equivalent (plus those 4 O-levels, including English and mathematics), can apply for entry into the bank's management training programme after 8–9 months' work in the bank, and after a number of interviews and aptitude assessments.

Starting salaries are from just over £3,000 for a 17-year-old entrant to between £3,500 and £4,000 for an 18-year-old, plus any London or large town allowances (£1,725 for central London, £298 for certain other big city postings). Staff can enter a contributory pension scheme at 20 (5 per cent of basic salary); other benefits include free banking, subsidized home and personal loans, interest free season ticket loans, an annual 2½ per cent bonus, plus a profit-sharing scheme. They work a standard 35-hour working week, with a minimum of 21 days' annual holiday rising to 30 days, plus bank holidays.

For further details, or an application form, contact:

The London Recruitment Office
Lloyds Bank PLC
Black Horse House
78 Cannon Street
London EC4P 4LN

Or write to 'The Regional Personnel Manager, Lloyds Bank PLC at whichever of the following addresses is nearest your home:

Rycote House
6 Temple Square
Aylesbury
HP20 2QG

PO Box 70
123 Colmore Row
Birmingham
B3 3AE

Bank House
Wine Street
Bristol
BS1 2AN

95–97 Regent Street
Cambridge
CB2 2AN

5 Cathedral Road
Cardiff
CF1 9HA

234 High Street
Exeter
EX4 3NL

Mount Manor House
The Mount
Guildford
GU2 5HS

PO Box 96
6–7 Park Row
Leeds
LS1 1NX

PO Box 358
Lloyds Bank Buildings
53 King Street
Manchester
M60 2ES

Black Horse House
91 Sandyford Road
Newcastle upon Tyne
NE1 8HQ

Market Square House
St James Street
Nottingham
NG1 6FD

PO Box 2
38 Blue Boar Row
Salisbury
SP1 6FD

Mount Pleasant House
Lonsdale Gardens
Tunbridge Wells
TN1 1NU

Graduates.   Lloyds operates a two-tier structure of graduate recruitment. It appoints around 60 Direct Entry Scheme applicants, and up
to 100 for its Alternative Entry Scheme.

Direct Entry is for honours graduates under 24 with 'high potential'. A two-speed training programme further divides the real high
flyers from their less evidently top-management-material colleagues.
A crash course in academic and practical banking enables the faster
of the two streams to reach junior management levels within 3 years
of entry and full branch management wihin 5. Beyond that, these

graduates are expected to form the core of Lloyd's future senior group management. The slower, more flexible training stream still aims for full management for graduates in their late 20s or early 30s.

The Alternative Entry Scheme is 'for those who have assessed themselves hard and feel they possess the wide spectrum of qualities required for branch management', but who do not want to join the high pressure programme of the Direct Entry Scheme. Graduates can, however, transfer to the accelerated programmes if they prove to be rather higher flyers than they thought.

Graduate starting salaries are approximately £7,600 for Direct Entry accelerated staff, £6,800 for those on the slower speed training course, and around £6,000 for those joining on the Alternative Entry Scheme. Allowances for London postings add £1,725 to the annual salary.

Specialist Careers for Graduates.   Lloyds takes around 4 graduates a year for its international division, 8 for its trust division and 8 for management services. No specific degree disciplines are required, although management services applicants should have some computer aptitude.

Pre-selection is on the basis of applications made before university visits (mid December to mid January).

For further information contact:

> The Manager
> Graduate Recruitment
> Lloyds Bank PLC
> Black Horse House
> 78 Cannon Street
> London EC4P 4LN

Midland Bank PLC

Staff: UK Banking 47,900; UK Group 67,065
Branches: 2,165 in Britain; branch banking subsidiaries in France, Canada, Australia, the United States and Switzerland.

The Midland Bank, founded in Birmingham in 1836, now ranks third of the 'Big Four' high street banks by number of branches and has a broad international business. It offers a full range of personal and business banking services; Access credit cards; travel services through its subsidiary Thomas Cook; merchant banking through Samuel Montagu; stockbroking through Greenwell Montagu; business and consumer finance through Forward Trust. Internationally, the Midland owns Germany's largest private bank as well as a number of other overseas branches. Its banking business is worldwide, through its own offices, and as a correspondent bank for 11,500 banking outlets in 186 countries.

School-leavers. The Midland appoints just over 3,000 school-leavers a year. Minimum qualifications for banking trainees are 4 GCE O-levels (grade C or above) or CSE equivalent, to include English language and mathematics. However, the Midland does take some secretarial staff with less than the minimum academic qualifications if they have a minimum typing speed of 35 words per minute, and shorthand of 80 words a minute. Suitably qualified people who have been working for a few years in other companies may be considered for secretarial openings nationally.

Banking trainees with GCE A-levels or their equivalent have 'a definite advantage' over their O-level colleagues. Outstanding recruits expecting to get at least 3 A-levels can apply for the 25 or so openings for the Midland's university studentship scheme. They join the staff for a year's accelerated training, and then enter the 3-year Banking and Finance degree course at Loughborough University of Technology on a normal local authority grant. Vacation work in the bank is at full pay. Students on this scheme receive a further 3 years' accelerated training, and have prospects of promotion to management grade by their early 30s. Applications for the university student scheme close on 30 September each year.

Other school-leavers may opt for clerical and junior banking work within the Midland's branches and offices, and the more ambitious can compete for places on the management training programme.

This offers a 6-8 year programme of in-branch and academic training leading to the first rungs of the management ladder.

Starting salaries for a junior aged 17 or under range from just over £3,000. An A-level entrant might expect a basic starting salary of around £3,500. Central London allowances add up to an additional £1,725 a year, and there is an allowance of £298 for staff working in most other major cities. Staff work a standard 35-hour 5-day week, with a minimum of 21 days' holiday, plus bank holidays. They are eligible for non-contributory pensions, reduced home and personal loan schemes, profit-sharing and annual bonus.

For further information or an application form, contact:

> Central Recruitment Office
> Midland Bank PLC
> Head Office
> 27/32 Poultry
> London EC2P 2BX

Graduates The Midland appoints around 90 graduates a year for its domestic banking, international banking and major non-bank UK subsidiaries. Maximum graduate entry age is normally 25.

There are no degree subject preferences for the 25 or so general banking recruits. The Midland's training programme involves a combination of in-branch practical work, training courses and study for the Institute of Bankers examinations. After 1½–2 years, graduate trainees are either selected for Special Grade accelerated training or, exceptionally, remain in the general training programmes with the prospects of eventual, but slower, promotion to junior or middle management.

Special Grade trainees spend a further 1½–2 years on more technical aspects of banking work, and completing the full Institute of Bankers' qualifications. All trainees are constantly assessed by personnel and branch or department managers. In the bank's words, 'banking is not a conveyor-belt career. There is no room for apathy, paper shuffling, or drifting. Only the front runners make an impression . . .'

Graduate starting salaries range from £6,500 to £7,000, plus regional allowances. Graduates are eligible for the full staff benefits, including the 2½ per cent annual bonus.

Specialist Careers for Graduates.   The Midland appoints around 20 graduates a year from all degree disciplines for work within its international banking business. Integration of the bank's domestic and international sides increases the similarities in selection and training programmes. Special Grade graduates complete a 3-year training programme either with UK-based international branches or at the international division's headquarters in London. On completion of that programme, and after successfully passing the Institute of Bankers examinations, graduates can expect a British-based (probably London-based) career with the possibility of brief secondments overseas, or business trips abroad. Staff do not normally work abroad for any length of time.

For further details contact:

> The Manager
> Personnel Planning and Development
> Midland Bank PLC
> International Division
> 110–114 Cannon Street
> London EC4N 6AA

A further 20 or so graduates are appointed to work within the bank's Group Management Services division. Most of the successful applicants have a degree in mathematics, computer science or similar disciplines. Graduate trainees join the Midland's central computer base in Sheffield as programmers, and careers within the Group Management Services, while offering the same pay and conditions as general domestic or international banking, may be spent working on the maintenance and development of the bank's computer systems, away from any direct customer contact.

Further information from:

> The Personnel Manager
> Group Management Services
> Midland Bank PLC
> Griffen House

41 Silver Street Head
Sheffield SI 3GG

Around 6 graduates are appointed to Group Treasury department
each year, to join a London-based group dealing with the central
money management of the bank at home and internationally. MBA
students, or those with good honours degrees in economics, mathematics, business studies, commerce, or other subjects requiring a
reasonable level of numeracy, are preferred. Training is more specialized than in general banking, and is tailored to individual graduates' strengths.

Further details from:

> The Personnel Manager
> Group Treasury
> Midland Bank PLC
> Suffolk House
> 5 Laurence Pountney Hill
> London EC4R 0EU

One or two law graduates are appointed each year to join the
Midland's Trust Company, which deals with wills, trusts, settlements, investments, income tax and custodianship of investments.
A 4-year training course, including study for the Institute of Bankers
Trustee Diploma, leads to a career primarily in the specialist trust
side of the bank's work. This specialization does not prevent pro-
gression across to branch management, or to senior management
within the bank.

Further information from:

> The Personnel Manager
> Related Services (UK Banking)
> Midland Bank PLC
> 47 Cannon Street
> London EC4M 5SQ

In an expansive year as many as 15 graduates, with no specific degree
preferences, may be needed to join the Midland's finance house
Forward Trust. Forward Trust is one of the country's largest finance
houses, providing point-of-sale finance for such things as cars and

washing machines, and, at the other end of the scale, the money for industries to buy anything from a shipping fleet to the machinery for a vehicle production line.

A sales-based training programme includes study for the Institute of Bankers examinations.

Further information from:

> Graduate Recruitment
> Personnel Department
> Forward Trust Group Limited
> Broad Street House
> 55 Old Broad Street
> London EC2M 1RX

Some 5–6 graduates each year join Midland's travel organization, the Thomas Cook Group. This is the largest multinational travel business, dealing with over 10 million customers a year, and with branches in 145 countries.

Graduates from most disciplines are considered for 2-year management training programmes, either on the retail side, dealing with Cook's individual and business holiday sales, or in product development, involved in the marketing and development of Cook's package holiday business. There is also a major financial services side, which deals with the issue of travellers' cheques – Cook's is Europe's largest issuer of travellers' cheques, and the world's second largest (after American Express).

The bank's holiday subsidiary makes this point: 'If your interests are mainly concerned with a desire to practise your languages and travel the world, *please do not apply*.'

Applications are made either on the bank's general graduate entry forms, marking your preference for work with the Thomas Cook Group, or, if you can present 'convincing reasons' for wanting to make a career there, you can ask for an application form and further information directly from:

> The Group Training and Development Manager
> Thomas Cook Group Limited
> PO Box 36
> Thorpe Wood

Peterborough
Cambs PE3 6SB

National Girobank

Staff: UK Banking 5,665
Branches: 21,663 (Post Office branches)

National Girobank is one of the youngest of the country's clearing
banks, having been established in 1968. Yet it has more high street
and side street outlets than all the rest of the banks combined, thanks
to its use of Post Office branches. National Girobank offers a full
personal banking service, including Visa credit cards, a fast-growing
national network of automatic teller machines (LINK) and as yet
restricted personal loans. Business services range from company
payroll management to money market investments, plus loan and
leasing finance and foreign exchange dealing. The bank, although
it uses Post Office premises and staff for counter work, operates
separately as a wholly owned but independently managed subsidiary of the Post Office.

School-leavers.   National Girobank's operational centre at Bootle,
Merseyside, and its 6 other regional offices across the country,
appoint clerical staff on an 'as and when' basis. There has been such
a rapid change in the scope of National Girobank's business in the
past few years, with the development of customer services to match
the traditional high street banks, that staff requirements have been
constantly changing.

   As counter work is dealt with by Post Office staff in the branches,
clerical recruits to one of the National Girobank's offices work
behind the scenes, keeping the heavily computerized accounts system operating and dealing with the normal administrative work of
a bank head or regional office. The bank tends to prefer school-
leavers with a certain amount of office experience, and its offices
regularly recruit experienced computer keyboard staff for machine-
operating jobs.

   Starting salaries for clerical assistants range up from around £4,000

a year, plus big city allowances where necessary. At the top of the
pay range a more senior clerical officer's salary would be between
£7,500 and £8,500, plus any locational allowances and overtime payments. Fringe benefits are more limited than in the other major
banks, primarily because National Girobank does not yet offer a
home loan facility. There are no low-cost loan facilities, although
staff do share a productivity bonus each year and the contributory
pension scheme is index-linked.

Scan local newspaper advertisements for job opportunites, or
write for more details, or to ask to be considered for future openings,
to the Staff Manager of your nearest National Girobank office:

> National Girobank
> 10 Milk Street
> London EC2V 8JH

> National Girobank
> Bootle
> Merseyside GIR 0AA

> National Girobank, Scotland
> 93 George Street
> Edinburgh EH2 3JL

> National Girobank, North East Region
> Merrion Court
> 44 Merrion Street
> Leeds LS2 8JQ

> National Girobank, North West Region
> 40–46 Dale Street,
> Liverpool L2 5TZ

> National Girobank, Midland Region
> 58–62 Hagley Road
> Birmingham B16 8PE

> National Girobank, South East Region
> Charter House
> Park Street

Ashford
Kent TN24 8EH

Graduates. Recruitment of graduate management trainees has changed in recent years. Instead of the traditional 'milk round' trawl of would-be bankers, National Girobank has tended to shift towards the appointment of graduates with 1 or 2 years' work experience in specific fields.

There are around 40 management trainee jobs to fill within the bank each year. But the expansion of the business banking side of National Girobank is creating an increasing role for the bank services 'salesman', paralleling the traditional role of the bank branch manager in taking his or her bank's services out to the corporate customer and trying to win new business. Rather than field a mass of generalist bankers, National Girobank's recruitment reflects a policy of appointing graduate salespeople for selling work, graduate accountants for accounting, and so forth. This specialist recruitment does not prevent graduates appointed to the bank from progressing up through their particular department or area of banking work to the more senior management of the business. And National Girobank's pace of growth suggests that the opportunity for promotion may well be greater than in the more mature high street banks.

Starting salaries for specifically appointed graduate specialists are fully comparable with equivalent rates in other British banks, although as yet without the broad range of fringe benefits.

Specific graduate recruitment advertisements appear from time to time in the national press. The bank makes the point that there are very many speculative applicants for a limited number of jobs. But for further information write to:

The Management Recruitment Manager
National Girobank
Bootle
Merseyside GIR 0AA

National Westminster Bank PLC

Staff: UK Banking 73,600; UK Group 82,499
Branches: 3,172 in Britain, a further 150 branches in the USA, and
international banking offices, subsidiaries or associates throughout
the world.

National Westminster has the largest British branch network of the
Big Four clearing banks. And it is one of the world's largest banking
groups, ranking in the international 'top ten' with direct banking
businesses, subsidiaries or associate banks across Europe, North
America, Australia and New Zealand, and the Middle and Far East.
In Britain it runs over 200 personal or business banking services,
from credit cards (Access) through to insurance broking; from hire
purchase to merchant banking, stockbroking and investment.

School-leavers.   Nat West appoints around 2,500 school-leavers a
year, and while there are no minimum qualifications as such, the
minimum for entrance to the Institute of Bankers examinations dis-
tinguishes purely clerical entrants from the potential young bankers.
It sets the basic minimum at 4 O-levels, including English language
and one quantitative subject such as mathematics, or the equivalent
CSE passes. Those with A-levels are appointed at a higher starting
career grade, and all school-leavers are encouraged to enter for the
Institute of Bankers examinations early in their careers.

   Starting salaries range from just over £3,000 for the youngest new
entrants. Staff work a 35-hour, 5-day week, with voluntary Saturday
morning work in some branches paid at a higher hourly rate. Staff
are eligible for a minimum of 21 days' holiday a year rising to 30
days, plus bank holidays. Benefits include non-contributory pensions, free banking, subsidized staff loans and home purchase loans,
interest-free season ticket loans, a share option scheme and a Christmas bonus of 2½ per cent of salary.

   Career prospects for school-leavers in Nat West depend upon success in the professional banking examinations, and on the bank's
assessments of performance. Clerical staff can reach management,
even senior management, grades in time, but today's graduate
entrants have a head start in the race to the top jobs.

For further information, and to arrange a local interview, contact:

> Recruitment Manager
> National Westminster Bank PLC
> National House
> 14 Moorgate
> London EC2R 6BS

Graduates. Between 200 and 250 graduates from all degree disciplines are appointed by Nat West each year, making it the largest graduate recruiter among the banks. Yet only around 1 in 25 applicants makes it through to the final selection.

. There are no restrictions on the degree disciplines of applicants, although the bank says that 'only candidates with an aptitude for, and a commitment to, a career in finance will be considered'. All graduate management trainees should be under 26 years of age.

Nat West pre-selects graduates for interview on the basis of their initial applications. Interviews are held during the university or polytechnic 'milk round', or at any time in London, or in one of the bank's area offices. Full day assessments of those who pass the initial interview can lead to a 2-day selection course for a limited number of special entry graduates at Nat West's own staff college, Heythrop Park in Oxfordshire.

The majority of the around 150 domestic and 50 international banking entrants join a 2-year management training programme involving branch and detailed banking experience, as well as work for the Institute of Bankers Examinations. After that period, assessments place the graduate bankers in a 4-speed career development scheme. Slow starters can move up to higher speed promotion tiers on later assessments, as high flyers can be reassessed down a tier if their performance doesn't match the pace or development expected. The top tier graduates get accelerated promotion, 'to give the opportunity to reach the highest positions within the bank'.

A strictly limited number of 'the best graduates in the country' can directly join Nat West's fastest speed promotion tier through its special entry scheme. Career prospects here imply the doubling of a starting salary of £7,500 (plus London or other big city allowances) within 5–6 years. These high flyers are expected to reach middle management by their mid 30s, senior management by their early 40s and an executive role within the bank before reaching 50.

For further information or application form contact:

> The Graduate Appointments Officer
> National Westminster Bank PLC
> Recruitment Department
> National House
> 14 Moorgate
> London EC2R 6BS

The Royal Bank of Scotland Group

The Royal Bank of Scotland Group was formed by the merger of the Royal Bank of Scotland and Williams and Glyn's bank in October 1985.

The Royal Bank of Scotland:
Staff: UK Banking 9,500; UK Group 16,900
Branches: 864

Williams and Glyn's
Staff: 6,800
Branches: 324

The Royal Bank of Scotland Group has overseas offices in North America, the Pacific Basin and Europe, and the group operates a full range of personal and business banking services at home and overseas, including the Charterhouse investment and stockbroking group.

School-leavers. The Royal Bank of Scotland Group appoints around 650 school-leavers a year. Minimum qualifications for banking staff to be eligible to entry for professional examinations set by the Institute of Bankers in Scotland or its English equivalent are: Scottish Certificate of Education with 4 passes at Higher grade, including English; or 3 Highers including English, plus 2 Ordinary grade passes; or the GCE O-level equivalents. Sixth-formers accepted by the bank who have either 3 GCE A-levels (including English), or two As and two Os can start on a higher initial salary grade.

Starting salaries rise from around £3,100 for the most junior new staff member. Training for professional qualifications and in practical banking is aimed at helping clerical staff to progress to sub-managerial and possible managerial positions. Success in Institute examinations is reflected in salaries, and in the pace of promotion.

Staff work a 5-day, 35-hour week, with a minimum 22 days' holiday, plus bank holidays, and permanent staff are eligible for free banking, subsidized home and personal loans, non-contributory pension, profit-sharing scheme, and a 2½ per cent Christmas bonus.

For further information or application form contact one of the following:

> The Staff Department
> The Royal Bank of Scotland Group PLC
> 42 St Andrew Square
> Edinburgh EH2 2YE

> The Personnel Department
> The Royal Bank of Scotland Group PLC
> New London Bridge House
> 25 London Bridge Street
> London SE1 9SX

> The Personnel Department
> The Royal Bank of Scotland Group PLC
> Mosley Street
> Manchester M60 2BE

Graduates. The Royal Bank of Scotland Group takes around 40 graduate entrants a year, pre-selecting candidates for interview in the 'milk round' of university and polytechnic visits from January.

No specific degree disciplines are called for, although 'a commercially based degree is an advantage'. A 3-year training programme combines branch experience with bank training courses and Institute examinations. Selected graduate trainees join the bank's

Programme, and 'it is from the pool of management development participants that most of the top jobs in the bank are filled'.

For further information or an application form contact:

> Recruitment Manager
> Royal Bank of Scotland Group PLC
> Personnel Division
> New London Bridge House
> 25 London Bridge Street
> London SE1 9SX

> The Personnel Manager
> Royal Bank of Scotland Group PLC
> Personnel Division
> 45 Mosley Street
> Manchester M60 2BE

> The Staff Manager
> Royal Bank of Scotland Group PLC
> Staff Department
> 42 St Andrew Square
> Edinburgh EH2 2YE

Trustee Savings Bank Group PLC

Staff: UK Banking 18,500; UK Group 26,665
Branches:1,600

The TSB Group was formed as a federal association of local savings banks, which were combined in 1976 as a centrally managed bank that has since become a publicly quoted company with 4 separate retail banking divisions: England and Wales; Scotland; Northern Ireland, and the Channel Islands. The TSB provides a full banking service, with personal loans and overdrafts, home loans, insurance, and the TSB Visa Trustcard, its charge, credit and cheque guarantee card. The group owns the United Dominions Trust instalment credit business.

School-leavers. The TSB recruits between 1,250 and 1,400 school-leavers a year through its regional offices. Ages: 16–21. Minimum qualifications are 4 GCE O-levels, including English language and mathematics, or 4 O grades in Scotland including English and arithmetic. However, the TSB makes allowances for staff who may be interested in cashier work, rather than aiming to progress through to management grades. 'When dealing with customers on the counter we think that personality is as important as academic achievement. So if you haven't got the necessary O-levels, we'd still be interested in speaking to you.' Recruits with 2 A-levels or 3 Scottish Highers have a head start in the TSB clerical grading.

Career prospects for the TSB staff have been improved by the pace of change in the bank in recent years. As this rapid switch from savings bank to fully fledged high street bank has been completed, fast promotions may be less common. But the TSB likes to promote internally, and provides in-bank training and time for staff to acquire Institute of Bankers qualifications. 'Promotions are awarded for ability, not length of service.'

For an application form, contact the Personnel Manager at

> TSB England and Wales
> 3 Copthall Avenue
> London EC2P 2AB

> TSB Northern Ireland
> 4 Queens Square
> Belfast BT1 3DJ

> TSB Scotland
> PO Box 713
> Orchard Brea House
> 30 Queensferry Road
> Edinburgh ED4 2UL

> TSB Channel Islands
> PO Box 70
> Curzon House
> Halkett Place
> St Helier
> Jersey CI

Specialist Careers for Graduates.   The TSB recruits a limited number of graduates, from any discipline but with an aptitude for computer work, for its computer services division which is based at Wythenshaw, near Manchester. The TSB Trust Company appoints a limited number of graduates to train in its insurance, unit trust and financial services operations, based initially at Andover, Hampshire.

Further details or application forms for pre-selection for interview from:

> The Graduate Recruitment Officer
> TSB Group Central Executive
> 25 Milk Street
> London EC2V 8LU

Yorkshire Bank PLC

Staff: UK Banking 4,861
Branches: 230

The Yorkshire Bank is the independently managed branch bank jointly owned by National Westminster (40 per cent), Barclays (32 per cent), Lloyds (20 per cent) and the Royal Bank of Scotland Group (Williams & Glyn's) (18 per cent). From its Leeds head office the bank's branches are spread through the North and the Midlands, with a branch in London. The Yorkshire provides a full personal and business banking service and issues Visa-based credit cards.

School-leavers
The Yorkshire Bank recruits around 250 school-leavers a year, although during a period of rapid expansion in 1983 and 1984 the number reached 600–700 a year.

Minimum qualifications for Yorkshire's general entry are 4 O-levels or equivalent (passed at one sitting), including English language and, preferably, mathematics. As around 200 of the bank's intake of 250 are 16-year-olds with these O-levels, the bank com-

ments that if banking really is the career you want 'it is without
doubt better to join the Yorkshire Bank at 16 rather than go on to
higher and further education', because there are more openings at
the junior level. Some 40–50 A-level entrants or BTEC National
Diploma/Certificate entrants are appointed as management development entrants.

Career prospects depend upon success in branch work, and junior
clerical staff are encouraged to take the professional banking examinations by correspondence course. Those who succeed in the banking examinations can progress to the management development
stream and aim for Associateship of the Institute of Bankers.

Starting salaries for the youngest new entrants range up from
around £3,150 a year. Staff work a standard 35-hour week, and have
free banking, non-contributory pensions and a profit-sharing
scheme.

Further details and application form from:

> The Manager
> Personnel Section
> Yorkshire Bank PLC
> 20 Merrion Way
> Leeds LS2 8NZ

Graduates.   The Yorkshire Bank appoints around 10–15 graduates
a year for its 2-year accelerated training programme. Graduates are
entered for Institute of Bankers examination courses, and are given
a crash course of banking experience in-branch and at Yorkshire's
training centre in Leeds. Graduate entrants are groomed initially for
branch management, and career prospects are broadly similar to
those in the other clearing banks, although the number of senior
management jobs in the Yorkshire is limited.

Further information from the Manager, Personnel Section (as
above.)

[The world of banking is in a constant state of change, and while
details relating to the main high street banks were accurate at the
end of 1987, do check the latest information with any bank you are
interested in joining before completing an application.]

12 The Merchant Banks

Britain's merchant banks provide services for companies rather than for individuals and, without the branch networks of the clearing banks with their large numbers of customer accounts, the merchant investment banks operate with small, highly professional staffs.

1. The Accepting Houses

The traditional three tiers of merchant banks have been blurred by the deregulation of financial services, with the acquisition of many of the long-established banks by giant combines. Long-established merchant banks in the City of London, whose business grew by accepting (adding their name to) bills of exchange issued by less well-known traders, were once able to raise finance more easily and less expensively than City financiers on their own.

The merchant banks needed to know enough about a wide variety of trading ventures to be able to judge whether a deal they were asked to add their name to in this way was a sound commercial risk. And this expertise, which City financiers relied upon as a form of credit reference, formed the basis of the City's merchant banking business.

In addition to finance for international trade, the merchant banks developed strong international currency departments, helping to raise finance for companies at home and abroad. Even as divisions of major groups they remain specialists in investment management for companies, for financial institutions such as pension funds and insurance companies, and for a few wealthy individual clients. They provide specialist financial advice, helping client companies, for instance, to raise capital on the stock market, or in takeover battles. And they deal in gold bullion, shipping, and increasingly in venture capital schemes, raising money for new companies to start and grow.

Staff numbers in the merchant banks which were members of the Accepting Houses Committee traditionally ranged from a few hundred to no more than 2,000. Job opportunities therefore were strictly limited, but the scope has widened as the volume of investment work in the UK has increased and as many merchant banks have become absorbed within financial conglomerates.

School-leavers
Applicants with a minimum of 4 GCE O-levels, including English and mathematics, are considered for junior clerical positions. School-leavers with 2 or more A-levels, or business studies diplomas, are also needed for clerical work at higher starting salaries. And there are occasional openings for those with good CSE passes and typing skills for machine-operating work. But even the larger of the merchant banks may take only 5–10 school-leavers each year. Many of the smaller banks have no school-leaver intake as such, appointing junior clerical staff as they are needed throughout the year.

Starting salaries are comparable with those of the clearing banks. Clerical staff usually work a standard 35-hour week, with 4 weeks' annual holiday. Non-contributory pensions are the norm, most of the banks offer low-cost home loan finance for longer-established staff, and profit-sharing schemes are common.

Career prospects for O- and A-level school-leaver entrants are far less clearly mapped out than in the major clearing banks. The merchant banks do not apply the kind of grading structures of the branch banks. They are, however, highly selective in their appointments, and the few school-leavers who do join merchant banks, and who gain the professional qualifications needed to move on from purely clerical work, may find promotions to responsible jobs come far sooner than in the clearing banks.

Applications may be made to the personnel managers of the merchant banks listed below (page 134), but bear in mind that only a few of the banks regularly appoint non-graduates, and that only a handful of really keen staff join each year. The take-over of merchant banks by financial conglomerates may also affect their independent, and, in the past, highly individualistic staff appointment policies.

Graduates

Size again limits the number of graduate entrants into merchant banking, particularly among the top, Accepting Houses Committee banks. Forty graduate entrants a year would have been a fair average for the 16 member banks, the largest taking under 10, the smallest only 1 or 2, if that.

The merchant banks tend not to have degree subject preferences, and while it is no longer entirely true to say that an Oxbridge degree and a 'blue' in an acceptable sport are pre-conditions of entry, the competition for jobs in the merchant banks is fierce. 'Average' candidates are unlikely to get to the interview stage.

Starting salaries are discreetly described as 'highly competitive' by the banks. Graduate entrants could expect to join on a salary of around £8,000–£8,500 in the banks' City offices. Training usually takes the form of brief initial familiarization programmes, combined with outside courses in such professional qualifications as the Certified Diploma in Accounting and Finance, a business school's Diploma of Corporate Finance or equivalent.

Career prospects for graduates are excellent. Fund management, corporate finance work or international banking offer early responsibility for major projects dealing at a senior level with corporate clients. Salaries have become internationally competitive, and are among the highest in the British banking community.

For further information, write initially to the Personnel Director of the investment banks listed below:

> Baring Brothers & Co. Limited
> 8 Bishopsgate
> London EC2N 4AE
>
> Brown, Shipley & Co. Limited
> Founders Court
> Lothbury
> London EC2R 7HE
>
> Charterhouse PLC
> PO Box 409
> 1 Paternoster Row
> St Paul's
> London EC4M 7DH

Robert Fleming Securities
25 Copthall Avenue
London EC2R 7DR

Guinness Mahon & Co. Limited
32 St Mary-at-Hill
London EC3P 3AJ

Hambros Bank Limited
PO Box 3
41 Bishopsgate
London EC2P 2AA

Hill Samuel & Co Limited
PO Box 20
100 Wood Street
London EC2P 2AJ

Kleinwort, Benson Limited
PO Box 560
20 Fenchurch Street
London EC3P 3DB

Lazard Brothers & Co. Limited
PO Box 516
21 Moorfields
London EC2P 2HT

Samuel Montagu & Co. Limited
PO Box 525
114 Old Broad Street
London EC2P 2HY

Morgan Grenfell
20 Finsbury Circus
London EC2M 7AS

N. M. Rothschild & Sons Limited
PO Box 185
New Court
St Swithin's Lane
London EC4P 4DU

Schroder Securities
120 Cheapside
London EC2V 6DS

Mercury International Group (inc. S. G. Warburg)
33 King William Street
London EC4R 9AS

2. *Other Merchant Banks*

Apart from the City's core of Accepting Houses Committee member banks, there are a number of other merchant banking houses carrying out similar corporate finance and investment work at home and abroad. Many of these other merchant banks are now subsidiaries of the major clearing banks, or subsidiary companies of other big corporations outside the banking world.

These merchant banks tend to be independently managed, and appoint their own staff for work primarily in and around the City of London, or on assignment internationally. Some of the clearing banks and merchant banks do, however, recruit through their parent company's staff system.

Here again, staff numbers tend to be small in comparison to the branch banks, and school-leaver and graduate entry and prospects are roughly similar to those in the Accepting Houses Committee banks.

For further information, write to the personnel director of one or more of the individual merchant banks, whose addresses you will find in the latest banking reference books, available at your local library.

3. *The Non-bank 'Merchant Banks'*

Many of the traditional merchant banking functions, and certainly most of their recently acquired roles in the provision of 'nursery' finance for new businesses and selection of new ventures to help launch new companies, are carried out by financial groups that are not formally banks. Since the 1979 Banking Act, the licensing authority of the Bank of England has accepted close on 300 businesses as 'licensed deposit takers'. These finance houses are seen to be sound, reputably managed, and able, in all but name, to act as corporate merchant banks or as retail banks in competition with the giant clearing banks of the high street. A number of these institutions evolved from, and retain their major business in, instalment credit for companies (leasing) or individuals (hire purchase). There are 43 member companies in the Finance Houses Association, many of the larger members being subsidiaries of the clearing banks. Among the merchant venturing licensed deposit takers – the non, but near, banks – there are school-leaver and graduate opportunities broadly similar to those in the top merchant banks.

For further information, write to the personnel managers of some of the larger merchant 'banks' – addresses from your reference library.

Many of the world's major banks and financial institutions have merchant banking subsidiaries which are also based in London (see the next chapter).

13 International Banking

The jet-setting world of the international banker is not all myth. And British bankers are uniquely well placed to enter that world. Language, tradition and time combine to make Britain a good launching pad for would-be international bankers.

English is the world's financial language. The English may well be spoken with an American or Japanese accent, and be jammed solid with money market jargon, but it's English all the same.

Tradition left the foundations of a world financial marketplace in the City of London after the Empire faded and Britain's commercial dominance of world trade ended. Like the docks, the international banks could easily have accepted their own decline and have become no more than a memory of past glories. Instead, the big high street banks used their home-based financial muscle to build or buy into branch banks elsewhere in the world; the merchant banks used their international expertise to develop new markets, to become exporters of their financial services rather than relying upon their customers to take them abroad; the world's banks started to congregate in the City as a civilized and well serviced home from home . . . and time provided a magnet that has made the City a more active financial centre than at any time in its history.

Time is money. And, for the international banks, London's position on the world time zones makes it one of the three pillars of the world money, alongside New York and Tokyo/Hong Kong. International traders deal from London with Tokyo in the mornings, and with New York in the afternoon; the world market follows the international telecommunication links around the globe. It never closes.

The result is that British banks rank high in the world ratings of international finance. Our major clearing banks stand alongside the giant, but far more domestically inclined, banks of the United States and Japan. City merchant banks, tiny in terms of staff numbers, stand equal in international financial services to the colossal finance houses of the States and Japan, and the financial arms of the Hong Kong trading companies.

East meets West in London as well. The state banks of the Iron Curtain countries cluster, as commercially minded as any Wall Street trader, alongside the classically capitalist financial institutions in the City. And these communist state banks are as adept at international money market trading as any western corporation with shareholders to please and a profit margin to maintain.

The City is host to nearly 300 overseas banks, by far the largest concentration of multinational money traders anywhere in the world. The representative offices of these overseas banks, the international divisions of the big domestic banks, and the London bases of the international banks provide several distinct career opportunities for would-be bankers.

Overseas Banks in Britain

Representative Offices

There are more than 160 overseas banks with representative offices in Britain. Most of those banks are content with a relatively small staff in office space as close as possible to the banking centre of the City of London. A further 50 overseas banks have set up their own full-scale branches in London to provide financial services for their own customers doing business in this country, as well as acting as a base for the banks' London money market trading. A few of these longer-established overseas banks have begun to spread their services into the British domestic market itself. Others have only a shared base in Britain, by maintaining a stake in a consortium banking operation with a number of other foreign, or local bank partners.

Most of these banks appoint some local staff – from a handful of secretaries and messengers to full teams of clerical, managerial, and executive banking staff hired and trained locally, or poached from British banks.

At the minimum, overseas banks coming to Britain provide work for the various professionals who are needed to ease their way into the country: the accountants, lawyers, estate agents and banking

consultants who find accommodation, present necessary information to the Banking Supervision Department of the Bank of
England, and evaluate potential costs, tax and so forth. At this stage
most overseas banks merely send their own staff to Britain to appoint
local advisers and to report back.

Once a first stage representative office is established, the overseas
bank tends to send in a general manager from its head offices to
organize the appointment of local staff. As overseas banks' representative offices are not permitted to deal with the public, and can only
do business with other banks in Britain, there is no need at this stage
to appoint a significant number of junior staff.

Very few overseas banks' representative offices will take on
untrained banking staff, other than messengers, purely clerical staff,
doormen, liftmen, cleaners, etc. Banking appointments are made
either by approaches to local career bankers who are personally
known to the overseas bank's representative – tapping the international old boys network – or through executive search companies,
the professional 'headhunters'. Junior banking staff are usually
appointed through direct advertisements in the London newspapers, adverts that will usually specify banking experience, or
through specialist employment agencies.

Salaries for 'poached' banking executives can be temptingly high.
The overseas bank may have no more than 6–12 staff based in
London, most of whom may be seconded from the bank's home
country. Appointing a senior British banker with good City contacts
is a way of cutting into the mainstream of British banking life fast,
so a salary package pitched well above local pay and benefit levels
can be a comparatively cheap investment for the incoming bank.
This growing enthusiasm among the overseas banks for poaching
the domestic banks' high flyers does not, however, extend down the
professional grades to the junior level. There, the British staff of
overseas banks tend to be offered much the same pay and conditions
as those found across the banking industry – the same salaries, the
same pension scheme arrangements, the same loan facilities, holidays and general conditions of service as the British high street
banks.

Branch Banking

Opening a British branch, with the ability to provide services for both British and overseas customers and their fellow banks, involves the overseas banks in a broader local recruitment programme. But here again, only a limited number of the biggest of the foreign banks have been established long enough, and have sufficiently wide ambitions, to develop their British banking businesses to appoint school-leavers or graduate trainees.

Citibank, from its Park Avenue headquarters in New York, runs one of the world's largest banking empires. As a financial group it ranks higher in cash turnover and assets than a good number of the smaller states whose diplomats work across town in the United Nations Building. As a lender to governments, Citibank has its share of high-risk Third World debts, and Britain's stable domestic banking market makes a temptingly calm and profitable contrast to its other overseas trade. It is, therefore, planning a substantial expansion of its operations in this country, building on its near 80-year experience of the British market.

Citibank already has some 50 branches in Britain, and has talked of expanding that network fivefold over the next few years. It is also planning to sidestep the problems and costs of running a national branch network, with all the staffing and property expenses that involves, by adopting the latest money banking technology and by making full use of shared facilities with existing financial groups.

As the first foreign bank to be allowed to join the British cheque clearing house system, Citibank plans to become 'a major force in British banking'. It is actively expanding its business in home lending, credit cards, automated teller machine services (fitted directly into Citibank branches or through shared systems – the Funds Transfer Sharing consortium, LINK, which includes the machines of National Girobank, the Co-operative Bank, the Abbey National Building Society, the Yorkshire Building Society and Western Trust and Savings), and high interest cheque accounts.

All these moves point the way to a British business aimed at minimizing the number of costly full-scale bank branches while maximizing the amount of high value, and highly profitable, personal banking trade. That policy also, clearly, restricts the number of counter staff needed by Citibank in Britain. But it also means that the bank will be greatly expanding its backroom UK staff to help market and manage this growing business.

Citibank's UK operations are centred, under its 'Citicorp' title, at:

> Citibank House
> 336 Strand
> PO Box 78
> London WC2R 1HB

American Express (Amex) is far more than a travellers' cheque and credit card company, although its US $15 billion travellers' cheque sales a year and 20 million card holders worldwide have made it one of the biggest of the international financial services groups. Its banking business and broking division – which now includes the giant New York firm of Shearson Lehman Brothers – are building a major base within the City of London, and they are likely to become significant employers across the range of banking jobs, from clerical staff to specialist merchant banking and investment work.

At the moment American Express's International Banking Corporation is based at:

> 12/15 Fetter Lane
> London EC4A 1PT

Of the other international banks with branch networks, or plans for branch networks within Britain, most tend to rely upon their own nationals for management, appointing only the more junior clerical staff locally. The Bank of Ireland, for instance, with 25 branches in Britain and over 500 offices at home, has the pick of the Irish school-leavers and graduates to choose from for its management training needs. And with some 20,000 applicants for what in recent years has been as few as 100 trainee places, the Dublin-based group has no need to trawl for talent within the UK.

Nevertheless, overseas banks do recruit local staff occasionally. A keen watch on the jobs columns in the newspapers can reveal the occasional junior banking position, and clerical and computer staff agencies often have a banking section that specializes in providing part-time or full-time staff for these banks.

International Merchant Banks

In terms of staff appointments locally, by far the most active overseas banking businesses in Britain at the moment are those UK subsidiaries of international banks which have little direct interest in providing banking services for ordinary high street customers, and which have long outgrown their representative office status. These are, for the most part, the merchant and investment banks with UK stockbroker subsidiaries operating in the City alongside Britain's traditional corporate banking houses, the international money traders with sizeable foreign exchange dealing operations based in London, and the purely international banks, whose work parallels that of the international divisions of Britain's big high street banks, but which have their parent company head offices in New York or Paris, Hong Kong or Tokyo.

All these major banks with specialist operations in or centred on London appoint clerical and junior banking staff locally. Again, although their employment policies differ, most of the overseas banks match their standards of pay, working conditions, staff benefits and so forth to those of the British high street banks.

Staff tend to be paid the same starting salaries, with similar loan facilities, and to work the standard 35-hour, 5-day week. In most cases they can also expect similar pension and bonus arrangements.

It is rare, however, to find a junior clerical staff member appointed in Britain who succeeds in training up through the management ranks to a senior position within the bank's parent company. It is rare enough to rise through the ranks to the top positions in a British bank, and few junior clerical entrants are likely to anticipate a career that will take them to the president's chair of their overseas bank. But this distinction between the long-term career prospects for general banking trainees in British banks and those for general office staff within British subsidiaries of overseas banks is a point that the most ambitious O- and A-level school-leavers might bear in mind.

Graduate entrants, on the other hand, might regard a management trainee position in an overseas bank in Britain as a strong career possibility.

Competition for jobs is fierce. For example, J. P. Morgan, the prestigious Wall Street bank, can take its pick of the best UK graduates.

It does hire 'relatively few, and seeks out the best men and women with a diversity of skills, expertise and backgrounds'. The bank's corporate operations have expanded in London to include a sizeable international money market business, through its Morgan Guaranty subsidiary. And the bank has, incidentally, some of the finest office accommodation in the City of London.

Morgan 'welcomes future bankers with backgrounds in any academic discipline. We hire the individual – not the degree.' And for the handful of successful applicants there are high-pressure training programmes, including time at base in New York. Starting salaries are competitive with the best of the domestic banks' graduate entrant scales, and those scales of pay and benefits tend to rise faster and more steeply than their UK equivalents.

Further details about their wider corporate banking work from:

> Graduate Recruitment
> Morgan Trust Company
> Morgan House
> 1 Angel Court
> London EC2R 7AE

For further information about their international trading work contact:

> The Personnel Manager
> Morgan Guaranty Ltd
> PO Box 124
> 30 Throgmorton Street
> London EC2N 2NT

Among the other major international banks with sizeable London-based corporate banking offices (apart from state-controlled national banks, whose London operations tend to be run by their own nationals and a limited number of experienced UK professionals), there are similar, and similarly limited, occasional openings for graduate staff.

When contacting these banks, it helps if you give the personnel manager a brief career history and some explanation of your enthusiasm for a career in international banking. Individual banks have their own graduate and school-leaver entrant programmes, which vary year by year according to staff requirements. Check the addresses of the international majors in the latest banking reference books, available in your local library.

International Banking

Few banking jobs involve a career spent regularly travelling the world. Outside the international banking divisions of the major British banks, or the overseas banks – where a mix of occasional secondments overseas and business trips abroad might well involve a limited number of more senior staff travelling fairly regularly – there are only a handful of genuine 'international banking' career opportunities as such.

The international staff of the Hong Kong and Shanghai Banking Corporation are an exception to this general rule. The bank has a staff of 40,000, working in 1,000 offices in 53 countries. And it recruits a limited number of graduate trainees each year in Britain.

Graduates can come from any degree discipline, and must be under 25, unmarried (because of the amount of travelling involved), numerically competent, and with a facility for languages. They must also be able to pass the bank's medical fitness tests and be prepared to work permanently overseas.

For further information contact:

> The International Recruitment Controller
> Hong Kong and Shanghai Banking Corporation
> 99 Bishopsgate
> London EC2P 2LA

> Standard Chartered Bank
> 8 Bishopsgate
> London EC2N 4BQ

Glossary

ACCEPTING HOUSES Top merchant banks are members of the Accepting Houses Committee. What they 'accept' are Bills of Exchange which are negotiable trading items.

ACCOUNT In a bank you can hold a current account, from which you draw your daily needs and into which you inject funds; a deposit account for your savings, withdrawn only at agreed terms of notice; and various investment or other accounts which are now offered. On the Stock Exchange, the account is a 2-week period (3 over holidays and bank holidays) in which you buy or sell for settlement in the following account period. Once the account closes after your sale or purchase, the deed is done and payment must be made. Then, of course, there are company accounts, which are plain old bookkeeping accounts despite being wrapped in myriad complications, legal or otherwise.

ADVANCE Just another name for a loan.

AFTER HOURS Stock Exchange term for between 15.30, when the Exchange closes for dealings, and the next morning at 09.30 when it reopens. Deals go on being struck after hours.

AGM/ANNUAL GENERAL MEETING Legally an annual must for all companies. Mostly dull, just routine approval of dividend, election of directors and agreement of auditing fees. Mercifully brief, though history records some lively ginger groups protesting on behalf of shareholders who are notoriously tame people.

ANNUITY A regular guaranteed income bought with an insurance policy or a lump sum; or, in the case of self-employed people, their self-bought pensions.

APPRECIATION Increase in the value of an asset, share prices, etc. The 'in' word for going – or gone – up.

ARBITRAGE International trading of shares, gold, currency, etc.; of anything that can be bought more cheaply in one country than another because of currency movements. This applies to any trading where – in a nutshell – you buy cheap, sell dear.

ARIEL   Automated Real-Time Investment Exchange. A computerized version of the Stock Exchange started by a few merchant banks to allow big buyers and sellers to deal with each other, thus saving time and stockbroking commissions. Used by pension funds, unit trusts and similar institutions.

ARREARS   If you don't know, are you the right type for banking? Debts due and overdue.

ARTICLES OF ASSOCIATION   The rules of a company when formed. Covers things like how many directors, how many shares of various kinds, borrowing and lending limits, share transfer agreements, shareholders' meetings.

ASSET   Possession of realizable value, be it land, money, plant, machinery, buildings, home, debts owing. Often taken as security against loans.

ASSET STRIPPER   One who sells or strips a company's assets instead of putting them to use for the company's good.

ASSURANCE   Old-fashioned but still-used word in life insurance. Since death is inevitable, sums are assured to beneficiaries. That's sure. Insurance is less so, an uncertainty, and don't some of us know it.

AT THE BACK DOOR   The Bank of England's way of getting money or other help into places or institutions that need it. Sometimes done with cash, sometimes by juggling interest rates. When money market people do it their own way, they operate at The Front Door.

AUDITOR   The accountant or accounting firm that vets the books to certify that they are true and fair. Sometimes he/they withhold certification or qualify the accounts with mild reservation.

AUTHORIZED CAPITAL   Capital a company can raise by selling shares as agreed by shareholders subject to minimum of £2. Can be increased by rights or other issues, but only with meeting of shareholders to approve such operations.

AUTHORITIES   Financially the Bank of England and the Treasury. Term little used outside banks, often inside them.

AUTOMATED TELLER MACHINES/ATM/CASH DISPENSERS, ETC.   We think you know these electronic cash dispensing machines.

AVERAGING Let's say your shares fall — sorry, depreciate. If you still have faith, still think they're going to be good, you buy more at the lower price, thus averaging the price downwards.

AVOIDANCE (OF TAX) Legal way of using the rules and the law to avoid paying tax. See also *Evasion*.

BAD DEBT An unpaid debt. Most debts carry a time limit, and then comes the assumption it is bad if still unpaid. Penalties can be anything from cutting off the gas, light or phone to whatever the courts may decree in the worst cases.

BALANCE What's left in your account after meeting all debts, paying all bills, honouring all commitments. Residue of a debt still owed.

BALANCE OF PAYMENTS The difference between what a country exports and receives in payment or what it imports and owes. There are invisible exports/imports such as tourism, expertise, insurance banking advice, etc. Visibles cover goods.

BALANCE SHEET The accounts that show the true position of a company, with liabilities on the left and assets on the right.

BALTIC EXCHANGE London's main shipping market, also trading in some commodities like grain.

BANK GIRO A system for transferring money between banks. Not to be confused with National Girobank, the state bank.

BANK OF ENGLAND The Old Lady of Threadneedle Street. The nickname came from a cartoon of the Napoleonic Wars, which depicted an old lady sitting on her chest of gold and trying to guard it from the grasping and pleading of Pitt the Younger, the Prime Minister, who wanted to finance the War.

BANK RATE Outmoded phrase for old scheme replaced by unimaginative, unsnappy but different Minimum Lending Rate. Died in 1981, but until then very much used as a manipulator by the Bank of England. All other bank rates being tied to it, the Old Lady could make lending easier or harder according to the instructions of her master, the government.

BANKING REVOLUTION Media phrase for slow move of banks into the twentieth century, less used since banks speeded their progress.

BANKRUPT Person unable to pay debts, so that his money or goods are managed by law to be used for the benefit of those to whom money is owed (the creditors). Though it is a popular word for 'broke', it actually applies only after the debtor is taken to court by the creditors. Not used for companies which are liquidated or in receivership.

BARGAIN   No such thing, of course, but actually the word for Stock Exchange deals. Those prices you see in newspapers are – allegedly – bargain prices, the prices at which deals are struck.

BASE RATE   Each bank's structure of interest rates. A bank normally pays about 2 per cent below base rate (usually called just 'base') on deposit accounts, but charges borrowers much more – anything from 1½ to 5 per cent more. Or even more. Pretty similar from one bank to another.

BASIC RATE TAX/STANDARD RATE TAX   The basic rate (28p in the pound in 1986–7) for low and average to medium incomes. Goes up to 60 per cent at the top rate, though it has been much, much higher before the last decade.

BEAR   A Stock Exchange pessimist, a seller of shares convinced of bad news ahead or of falling prices.

BEARER BONDS   Certificates of ownership of bonds or shares that can be transferred from seller to buyer without formal deeds or re-registration.

BELOW THE LINE   Favourite Chancellor of the Exchequer phrase when presenting budgets. Payments and receipts for or from nationalized industries, public works, etc. The government's fixed costs. Often used, wrongly, as synonym for Bottom Line, the profit line. Above the line, government-wise, go current commitments and contingencies.

BENEFICIARY   Of a will, insurance fund, etc. One who benefits.

BID   Shares and other traded commodities are quoted in two prices, the bid price and the offer price. The one you pay when buying is naturally the higher of the two, the offer price. When you sell it will be at the lower bid price. Also takeover bid, by which one company tries to acquire another by bidding a tempting price for shares.

BILLION   Used to be the most fantastic, enormous sum, a million times a million. Some years ago we in Britain adopted the American version, in which a billion is a thousand million. Now standard at the Treasury and elsewhere.

BLUE CHIP   First-class, top-quality share. Safe. Examples – ICI, Marks & Spencer, etc.

BOARD   Of directors or governors, a collection of elected people who run businesses, schools, charities, government agencies, quangos, etc.

BOND   A promise to pay over an agreed time from government, company, insurance firm, local authority, anyone licensed so to do. You can get interest while you wait for the capital to be redeemed.

BONUS   Extra sum. Sometimes agreed, often not; paid by employers (normally at Christmas), insurance companies (if they earn enough) and for being good (by parents). Bonus comes from the Latin meaning good, a good thing. A plus over what is due. A bonus share issue is not really that. You seem to get free shares but watch the price fall so that your total holding remains the same. If you get a one-for-two bonus issue you end up holding three shares for every two you formerly owned. The total, combined price of the three is probably very much the same as the combined price of the 'old' two shares.

BOOM   The opposite of slump or depression or, as the more modern call it, recession. Alas, like slump, often temporary, though some post-war booms have gone on for a long time. As they put it in *Porgy and Bess*, 'when the livin' is easy'. Turnover, employment incomes, output, all rise. By the way, so do prices.

BOUNCE   What a cheque does when the account is far from booming. If there are no funds to meet the cheque, the bank bounces it back to the payee's bank, who bounce it to him suggesting he Refer to Drawer (often abbreviated to RD).

BOURSE   The French Stock Exchange. Name also used for some other European exchanges.

BRADBURY   The bank note used by your grandfather or other ancestor. All bank notes issued between 1914 and 1919 were signed by the then Secretary to the Treasury, John Bradbury, and the notes took his name.

BREAK-UP VALUE   The value of a company's assets minus its liabilities and compulsory commitments, preference stocks, etc. Finding out is an arithmetical exercise beloved of predatory takeover bidders, who want to get their victims on the cheap with all expenses paid from the victim's purse. A phrase often used by commentators on companies and finance.

BRIDGING LOAN   A loan to bridge the gap between the need and the realization of some promised sum. Often related to home-buying. Banks are usually kind about this, helping with the costs and expenses of buying the new home before selling the old because they realize it will all resolve itself in time.

BROKER   A commission agent, an agent who deals for you in shares, commodities, currency, goods, in return for commission. A middleman.

BUDGET   The government's corporate plan for the year ahead, with details of spending, commitment, revenue and income. Always announced in the spring, usually before the end of the fiscal year (4 April). Presented by Chancellor of the Exchequer, who gives a half-term report around November.

BUDGET ACCOUNT   With banks, stores, gas, electricity, telephone, etc.; an agreement to pay so much per month against inevitable bills. With the bank, an agreement to pay regular monthly sums into the budget account from which they handle major bills for you.

BUILDING SOCIETIES   Financial organizations that take deposits on which they pay interest but which exist mainly to lend money as mortgages for people to buy homes or commercial property. Fascinating history, as they grew from groups of enterprising individuals pooling their own resources and drawing lots to see who got the money for a plot of land. Then all went on paying until another plot could be afforded, and lots were again drawn. Now the societies are very sophisticated; they carry out a lot of the same functions as the clearing banks and are more or less rivals.

BULL   The optimist of the Stock Exchange. Bulls expect prices to rise. Brave and perhaps foolhardy bulls buy a share, convinced it will rise, hoping to sell inside the account so that they never have to pay for the shares but receive only the profit. Often caught having to find the money.

BULLION   What a lovely word for gold or silver. Old-fashioned, implying only the purest unalloyed precious metal. In bars, ingots or such, not as *objets d'art*.

BUSTED BOND   A loan to government on which interest has ceased to be paid. Gamblers buy them in the hope that interest will be revived which, in the dim and distant past, it occasionally has been. Britain has never been guilty but other countries . . . well who's naming names? No good.

CAPITAL   Assets, be they cash, property or a business – anything as long as it is readily saleable. Money used in a business. More varieties than Heinz, but accountants' descriptions mean much the same despite their sophisticated and varied names for capital.

CAPITAL GAINS TAX OR CGT   Born in 1965 under Labour's James

Callaghan, it takes 30 per cent of any capital gain on shares, paintings, jewellery, houses, etc., with the exception of your owner-occupied home, your car, gambling wins, gilt-edged stock, pension lump sums, life insurance policies, etc. You are entitled to a CGT-free annual allowance which is index-linked, more or less.

CAPITAL TAX A very different thing, meaning tax on wealth. Not yet introduced, thank goodness, but prevalent in some countries and often lobbied here. But look at the next item.

CAPITAL TRANSFER TAX - CTT A tax on cash or gifts made in your lifetime or at death. Transfers between spouses are exempt, and there are generous annual allowances, wedding gift allowances, charity donations and such.

CAPITALIZATION ISSUE/SCRIP ISSUE Already outlined under *Bonus* (bonus issue). Shares apparently but not actually given to shareholders when company reserves have grown disproportionately to share capital or share prices become unwieldly.

CARTEL A sales 'ring', a consortium of members having an interest in there being an agreed combined output. The object is to control supply and demand and thus also to control rarity value and prices. Note De Beers and diamonds, of which sales are strictly rationed.

CASH Come now, we all know what that is.

CASH COW A business that may not yield big profits but which generates plenty of ready money. Newspapers are prime examples. In conglomerates, useful to have because cash can be used in other more profitable divisions.

CASH FLOW The money that flows from trading to be reinvested in the business for new assets, working capital, etc. Going in, it is positive cash flow. Going out, it is negative.

CASH PIG Opposite end of cash cow, a business or division that eats up the money.

CAVEAT EMPTOR Latin for 'let the buyer beware'. Consumerism has done much in recent years to protect the consumer from his own mistakes, so he might beware rather less than he should. He should not come to rely too much on protection which is not always there.

CENTRAL BANK Here in the UK, the Bank of England. The bank in any country that acts or manoeuvres to carry out government's ploys to control the money supply.

CHEQUE   The piece of paper, printed with your bank's name, that is your promise to pay the sum you write on it. Actually, people have written cheques on all sorts of strange things, from menus to footballs, and there is even a tale of a man writing one on a valuable ostrich egg. Banks may charge quite a bit to negotiate such strange cheques.

CHEQUE CARD   The card issued by your bank to guarantee that the cheque will not bounce, but will be met up to a ceiling figure. You cannot stop cheques given with a cheque card, so watch it. Gradually, as electronic devices appear at shop and other retail outlets, the card will be less and less needed.

CIF   Cost, insurance, freight. Prices for shipped goods are quoted CIF, meaning that the seller pays all such costs up to the goods being on board. Buyers who can handle these costs for themselves at lower prices should buy FOB (Free on Board).

CITY   Once, and theoretically still, the Square Mile containing the Stock Exchange. The City has spread. Read all about it in books or leaflets from the Information Department, Corporation of London, Guildhall, London EC2P 2EJ.

CLEARING BANKS   If you have read this book, you know. Banks which are members of the system that clears cheques through the clearing house, where millions of scraps of paper (cheques) are swapped and sent on to their proper destinations – i.e. your cheque to your bank and pretty fast at that.

COLLATERAL   What your bank manager wants if he is to approve a loan or overdraft. The security he seeks can be anything from insurance deeds to house deeds (which you won't have unless you've paid off the mortgage), stock and share certificates, that kind of asset. They will be valued by the bank at – very roughly – about two-thirds of the current market value in case some disaster happens.

CONGLOMERATE   A company of all-sorts, all mixed up together and operating under one great big parent company. Different divisions within the group may make or serve anything, for example hosiery, engineering parts, construction services, chemicals. Together they form a conglomerate. The idea is that good times for some cushion bad times for the others. In truth, few conglomerates fly high because there are always bad times for some parts of the group. The mirror to that is that they rarely slide downhill fast, but they have done. Banks fear them. When a company is absorbed by a conglomerate, one of the things that tends to be rationalized is the banking system, and the new boy may in time come under the parent's bank. Not always, but it happens pretty often. This kind of takeover is sad for the bank, which probably helped the young one along to the greatness and goodness that made the big daddy covet it.

CONSUMER DURABLES Merchandise that lasts some time, such as washing machines, furniture.

CONTANGO An arrangement to carry over and delay payment for your shares. As a bull, you bought expecting prices to rise. They didn't, and you can't pay, but you still think they will rise so you don't sell (anyway they may have gone down and you don't want the loss). You pay your stockbroker a fee for them to be contango'd.

CONVERTIBLES Not sexy cars, despite what Dr Dichter said. Financially, stocks/shares carrying the right or option to convert into other kinds of stocks/shares in the same company.

CONVEYANCING The legal name for transferring title of property one to another.

CORNERING Buying up as much as possible of a certain commodity to build yourself a monopoly and then be able to charge what you like for the stuff. Rare to the point of non-existence these days; much done in the 1920s and 1930s.

CORPORATE FINANCE Company finance, the kind often handled by merchant banks.

CORPORATION TAX Tax on company profits, another of James Callaghan's reforming introductions in 1965. Until then companies had paid income tax on similar lines to individuals.

COUPON Nominal rate of interest on a fixed-interest stock, based on the stock's nominal capital value (in government stocks, always £100). You may get a better or worse yield depending on the price you pay for the stock.

COVENANT A written and binding agreement; and conveniently one way of legally avoiding some tax. Strike covenants with your student children over 18, your nieces, nephews, grandchildren and all, and you will get the benefit of their collecting tax-free allowances equivalent to the personal allowance. Thus they get £100 for every £72 that you give them – the government supplies the £28. Covenants must be for 7 years.

COVER Either how much a company has to cover its dividend once, twice or three times; or the sum an insurer promises on any policy.

CREDIT CARDS These first came to Britain via Barclays Bank in 1966, as they still emphasize in their advertising (among other firsts). Soon joined by Access, to which the other 'Big Three' subscribe. Now many others – shops and other banks have their own. All similar. The card can be used instead of cash to buy goods or services where the relevant signs are displayed. They can also be used to draw cash, from machines or over the counter. Monthly statements show what you owe, demand a minimum payment and spell out interest on what is unpaid. Expensive interest but virtually easy-come loans.

CREDIT UNION A group of friends, workmates or such set up their own union, each buying at least one £1 share. There must be a minimum of 21 members, a maximum of 5,000. Each can borrow from the union but must pay interest. The trouble is that there is a legal limit of 12 per cent chargeable interest while investors' dividends are pegged 8 per cent. Thus investors easily find better homes for their money. So they are scarce here, well known in Europe, hardly a threat to the banks. But building societies started from such small beginnings. Something could develop.

CREDITOR Someone who has given credit, who is therefore owed money or some form of negotiable currency.

CREDIT TRANSFERS Transfers via bank or similar institution to pass money from one to another without cash being involved.

CURRENCY Strictly and simply money; but usually the monetary units of countries. Thus francs, marks, dollars, lira.

CURRENT ACCOUNT The daily needs account; the one into which the salary goes, from which needed cash is drawn and against which the cheques are written. See *Account*.

CURRENT COST ACCOUNTING Call it CCA and you will be very 'into' finance. Born of rampant inflation in the 1970s, when accountants realized that profits were never going anywhere near to replacing anything new from paper clips to generators. So the accountants worked out the most compli-cated way of revealing these horrific costs to shareholders. For a long time firms presented accounts both in CCA and the old form, called historic accounting. Still all rather a dog's dinner, but settling down despite many disagreements between accountants themselves.

DAY BOOK The daily record of all transactions before these are sorted out and entered into various different accounting sections such as sales, pur-chases, overheads, fixed costs and so forth.

DEBENTURE   A loan to a company offering property as security. First loans to be repaid when the company is liquidated.

DEFLATION   What's that? Well, we have known it in the past and it means falling prices and costs. Also, alas, and in the inevitable truth of economics, falling incomes. If you're young enough to be job-hunting you may never even have heard of it.

DENARIUS   The only reason for bringing up this ancient Roman coin is that it was the 'd' of our old penny, the one that went when coin was decimalized in 1972. It actually meant 'ten asses' in Latin, and the l.s.d. of our old coinage stood for Libra (pounds), Solidi (shillings) and Denarii (pence). Useless knowledge, but it might impress when conversation runs out.

DEPRECIATION   Opposite of appreciation, a fall in value. In company accounts, loss from wear and tear, obsolescence, from any reason.

DEPRESSION   A slump, a recession (see *Boom*).

DEVALUATION   The act of reducing one's currency against that of another country. We in Britain did it several times vis-à-vis the US dollar, the exchange rate falling from 5 dollars to the £ until it came down to $1.80. In the 1970s it 'floated', and natural forces have devalued sterling often and ruthlessly since then. However, the stigma of one's currency weakening against other currencies is virtually gone. We've all had to live with rapid changes and we all survive.

DIRECT DEBIT   Like a standing order, a way of paying your bills or other financial commitments via the bank. You fill out a form that gives the gas, town hall, electricity or telephone people the right to take your money on a regular basis – usually monthly. Developed from standing orders, which required the bank to pay the same sum each month on the same day. Direct debit allows the payee to take variable sums, useful with building societies as mortgage rates change. Becoming somewhat less unpopular; liked by banks because there is less paperwork because the payee calls for his money. Take two precautions. Ask the payee company to advise you before they take any unusual sum or alter the agreed monthly sum; and give your bank a limit not too far above the said agreed sum. It should all be fine but things can get mixed up.

DIRECT TAXATION   Taxes paid directly to government, for example *Income tax*, *Capital transfer tax*, etc.

DISCOUNT   A cut off the usual price. With shares, simply a fall in the price – you buy a new share, say, at issue price, and if it is not in demand, it may go to a discount. You pay your full price and take the discount if you sell. On goods and services, lower prices hence discount shops or stores.

DISCOUNT MARKET   In the City of London, a market dealing with Treasury bills, short-term gilts, bills of exchange, etc. Dealings are by phone with the discount houses approved by the Bank of England. All part of government policy on interest rates, a market that can be manoeuvred to ease rates down or stir them up a little. Discount bills are sold prematurely by the holder because he does not want to wait for maturity. The discount at which he sells is roughly the equivalent of the interest he loses by not waiting.

DISPOSABLE INCOME   What is left to spend after deducting all tax commitments, national insurance and any other mandatory payments.

DIVIDEND   The interest or share of profits that a company pays to shareholders for having the use of their money. Covered by the net profit of the company. If profits are less than dividends payable they are uncovered. A cover of three times or more is generally thought to be healthy. Cover is obtained by dividing pre-tax profits by pre-tax cost of the dividend.

DOUBLE TAXATION   Occurs when the taxpayer lives in one country but works in another. To prevent people paying tax in both places, most countries have double taxation treaties with each other so that taxpayers fork out only once in one country. The phrase can also describe the system of taxes to a central government as well as local taxes to a state, local authority, county or similar division of the country.

DOW JONES   The index of share prices in America, the counterpart of our own FT index. Properly named but rarely called Dow Jones Average.

DUMPING   The selling of goods at artificially low or subsidized prices. Countries, anxious to build their export trade, might do this to enter new markets and inhibit rivals. Bitter accusations were hurled at the Italians over washing machines, fridges and hosiery but none were sustained by proof. However, the Italians beat our own home manufacturers into the red too often for our health.

EMBEZZLEMENT   The theft of money from employer or client, usually by fraud and deception.

ENDOWMENT INSURANCE   Insurance to collect a lump sum at an agreed time after so many premiums have been paid.

ENDOWMENT MORTGAGE   Mortgage linked to endowment insurance so that a lump sum pays off the mortgage. Interest is payable on the loan meanwhile.

EQUITY   Ordinary shares. But you can own the equity in any asset – your daughter's house, your own business. You get the profit. Or the loss.

ERNIE   Electronic Random Number Indicator, a computer that picks Premium Bond winning numbers.

ESCROW   A state of suspension for money. If a contract takes time to fulfil, the buyer may put the money with a third party in an escrow account. Both sides know it will be paid, and the seller can get on confidently with making or preparing what he will then eventually sell without worrying whether the cash is due. Interest on the money normally belongs to the person whose money is lodged.

EUROBONDS   Traded by major companies. The bonds are in a named currency, normally the strongest at the time, floated on most European stock exchanges, then traded by banks and money brokers. Strictly for those who know what they're doing.

EURODOLLARS   Originally US dollars held by Europeans. Now the Eurodollar market deals in many differing currencies.

EUROPEAN COMMUNITY   The Common Market, which began in 1957 with the Treaty of Rome.

EVASION OF TAX   Illegal evasion of tax. See *Avoidance*.

EX   Ex-dividend, ex-rights, ex-capitalization. Shares that are ex no longer bear the rights named, and there is normally a drop in the price to take this into account. Abbreviations against the share price will read xd, xr or xc.

EXECUTOR   One who carries out the instructions of a will, then applies for probate.

FACE VALUE   The nominal value printed on any note, bond or other paper. By no means always the same as market value. That is geared to supply and demand.

FACTORING   A system whereby the factor lends money to a client against his flow of invoices. The factor gets the money against the invoices, then settles the differences. Often helpful to smaller firms because factors, especially when they are owned by the banks, have rather more muscle when it comes to calling in payments from dilatory payers. Small firms have too little muscle.

FED   The American central bank, the Federal Reserve Bank.

FINANCE ACT   Legal ratification of the Budget proposals. Normally comes in mid to late summer.

FINANCIAL TIMES   The FT, the British daily newspaper bible of the money business. Carries money news, share prices, everything to do with money.

FISCAL YEAR   The tax year. In Britain from 5 April to 4 April the following year.

FLOTATION   The launching of a company's shares on to the Stock Exchange or Unlisted Securities Market (USM) for the first time; the privatization of a nationalized industry.

FOB   Free on Board. See *CIF*.

FRANCHISE   A licensing system whereby an operator uses the trade names, secrets, recipes and systems of major companies, usually within an agreed area where there will be no direct competition. Most banks have specialist franchise advisory departments and will lend to potential franchisees provided they are hitching up with a respectable member of the British Franchise Association.

FRINGE BENEFITS   Benefits in kind, for example luncheon vouchers, the company car or moped, medical insurance, etc.

GARBLE   Inner sanctum banking expression, meaning to sort old notes due to be taken out of circulation. The old ones are returned to the Bank of England and burned at the Essex printing centre, where they form fuel for the hot water and central heating. The Great Train Robbery was a theft of garbled notes en route for burning. The £1 coin will eliminate a lot of garbling.

GAZUMPING   Offering to the seller more than the quoted price or the price already agreed with another buyer. The aim is to shut out the first offer. A word born in the 1970s property boom. It made people wonder about the fact that contracts for homes are exchanged so long after offers are made and accepted – change of mind is possible and legal within that period. In Scotland or at auction, the contract is immediate and binding.

GILT OR GILTS   Short for gilt-edged stocks, alias loans to government. Said to be safe, but don't be fooled. The government keeps its word all right and pays the interest on the due dates, redeeming the capital value also on the proper date. In between you can lose if you have to sell, because prices fluctuate like share prices, especially on undated stocks without clear commitment to repay. If we draw a veil over War Loan, which fell to the floor as the government failed to honour it though continuing to pay the interest, most gilts are OK. They fall into three categories: Shorts, redeemable in 0–5 years; Medium, for the 5–10 year stocks; and Longs, repayable in 10–15 years. All trust funds must by law have some of these. Banks, having been brought up on them, like them. Gilts can have their flying moments but good shares are often more rewarding. The trouble is finding the good shares.

GIRO A system initiated by the Post Office and later adopted by the banks, which simplifies the transfer of money. Originally set up to help people without bank accounts, it was cheap and simple to understand though many failed to do so. Now standard practice for paying bills, especially to the fuel utilities, the rates and such – the nationalized industries helped giro to get off the ground after its rocky start. No longer all that cheap, but cheaper than a lot of cheques-plus-postage-stamps. Less trouble too.

GLAMOUR STOCKS Not gilt-edged stocks but high flyer stocks, go-go shares, fast on the rise. Equally fast on the slide, it must be said, and collections of junk stocks today include many a high flyer of yesterday. Usually groups of industries that come suddenly into fashion, for example Australian mines in the early 1960s, currency broking in the late 70s/early 80s, electronics in the early 80s, and that kind of thing. Property was a real glamour stock in the late 50s/early 60s, but in time they faded and property itself became the glamour investment. The phrase implies doubtful, so beware.

GNOMES OF ZURICH Swiss bankers, whether they are in Zurich or not. Came into the language in the early 1960s, when sterling was in crisis and the gnomes were said to be cold, heartless manipulators out to destroy socialism and socialists (it is thought that Labour MPs coined the phrase). In some places, gnomes mean all European bankers but not those respectable, honourable, straight-bat British bankers. Happily the Swiss took it all with good humour, but the name stuck and moneyed men are often referred to as gnomes even if they are not bankers.

GOING PUBLIC Selling stock to the public, usually the launch of a private company on to the stock market. See *Flotation*.

GOLD In theory see *Bullion*. In practice often alloyed. At one time the hoard of gold owned by any country meant its wealth. Here in Britain, as in other countries, notes were once printed only when backed by gold to the value of such notes. Whenever we have tied our currency to gold, we have run into depression and recession. See the next item.

GOLD STANDARD   A dead phrase for a dead system of matching our issued banknotes to our gold reserves. In 1844, by royal charter, extra bank notes were issued and were called a fiduciary issue, but we stuck, in theory, to a gold standard for some time longer, gradually increasing the fiduciary issues until 1914 when we came off the gold standard. A brief attempt to restore it in the 1920s proved unsuccessful. The French believe in gold; the Americans guard it carefully underground at Fort Knox or below the Fed – see Fed. They say that each country's gold is stored in little alcoves and labelled; then each day, strong men push the ingots back and forth between the niches to tally with inter-country dealings in gold. It may happen, especially for films or TV. Most deals are paper deals, money is paper money. There is a dealing ceremony among London's bullion dealers when the gold price is fixed, such agreement between them being signified by the knocking over of tiny toy Union Jacks in front of the gold-fixing men.

GOLDEN HANDSHAKE   Compensation in cash or kind for being fired or for losing your job in any way that is patently not your fault. There are those who have had several, as a result of takeover bids for their companies, for failing to get the profits, for all sort of reasons. You don't have to be good at the job to get one – often the contrary. Rare in banking, where people are not often fired without good reason.

GOODWILL   The invisible of the balance sheet. It can mean expertise and know-how, patents, contacts, good customer lists, anything. Not beloved of auditors or shareholders. Permissible in service companies. Just. Nebulous, doubtful, dying away.

GOVERNMENT BROKER   The man through whom the government buys and sells its stocks, via the Bank of England. A partner in the broking firm of Mullens and Co., who works with the bank on day-to-day stock market ploys in gilt-edged stocks.

GRANNY BONDS   Index-linked National Savings bonds which were originally available only to the elderly. Launched in 1975. See *Index-linked*.

GREEN POUND   Common Market scheme for deciding prices under the Common Agricultural Policy (that's CAP). The relevant national currencies are taken out of context and marked at a fixed, not a floating, value and they are moved from that base only after long, involved discussions and negotiations. If the green pound is strong, butter is cheap but the farmers get paid less which makes them unhappy which . . . but no space to go on about all that here.

GRESHAM'S LAW   One of the famous economist theories that 'bad money drives out good'. The basis is that inferior money of nickel or paper will be used by people who will then try to hoard and hide good money of gold or silver. Gresham, who advised the first Queen Elizabeth more than 400 years ago, was something of a Canute about changing money patterns even then, though there is an interesting piece of financial history to support his catch-phrase. People still hoard golden sovereigns. It's a phrase often used in conversation even now.

GROSS   Opposite of net. Meaning the whole sum, with no deductions for tax, debts, bills, commitments, commissions, anything of that sort.

GROSS NATIONAL PRODUCT   Almost always called GNP. Notice it around Budget time and in various weighty commentaries on our economy. It is the total value at current or constant prices of our annual production of goods and services. The idea is that such value is available to the country for adding to or maintaining its material wealth. It's an economist's phrase, to describe the way they measure our national progress. Governments tend to use it as a measure of our productivity vis-à-vis other countries. It takes no account of other components of lifestyle and happiness.

GUARANTOR   One who guarantees somebody else's debt, for bank over-draft, hire purchase agreement or similar commitments. Guarantors are liable for any debt on which the borrower defaults, whether they are broke or not.

HAMMERING   This is what happens to a member of the London Stock Exchange who cannot meet his obligations (that's the euphemism for debts). The name of the defaulter is called out from a rostrum inside the Exchange and silence falls on the House. There is a fund to protect clients from the consequences of hammering, and hammering is itself rare nowadays. Often the fault of a major client who fails to pay.

HARD CURRENCY   Any stable, steady, reliable currency that is acceptable in world markets. British, Swiss, Dutch, German and such like are in the hard category. Roubles and other Iron Curtain currencies are soft.

HOLDING COMPANY   A conglomerate can be a holding company but not always vice versa. A holding company holds at least 75 per cent of the shares or securities of its subsidiary companies. Its main business may be simply holding shares, though it naturally exercises some managerial responsibilities even if only to interfere and to ask questions when things go wrong. Different from a conglomerate in that the latter normally owns 100 per cent of its subsidiaries and manages more closely – if it is possible to manage a whole lot of diverse businesses closely.

HOT MONEY   The money that rushes from country to country chasing the highest interest rates or other special circumstances that harden currency.

Hot money can disappear as fast as it comes if something more attractive turns up elsewhere, and countries dislike the hot money merchants, though occasionally finding them useful to tide them over rough spots. Solid steady investors are preferred.

INCOME   What you earn from work or investments.

INCOME TAX   The tax you pay on your income as distinct from other taxes – see *Capital gains tax*, *Capital transfer tax*, *VAT*, etc.

INCREMENT   An increase. Annual increments are yearly increases in salary or wages, sometimes built into agreements of employment. The object of such an agreement is to prevent or avoid the arrival of demands for more, more, more; and the strikes that go with refusal.

INDEMNITY   Compensation for loss, insurance term. If you're insured you are indemnified against something. There can be political indemnity, meaning exemption from certain legal penalties for breaking laws.

INDEX   There are many indices, as the plural has it. Cost of living index, wholesale prices index, retail prices index and so it goes on and on. Mostly shortened – the RPI will almost certainly be familiar to you. The index is the measurement of whether prices or whatever are rising or falling (but you may never have seen the latter).

INDEX-LINKED   What happens to some investments, some pensions, some wages, etc. When inflation began to take off in the 1970s people began to demand – and some got – wages and pensions that were/are index-linked. The government issued National Savings Certificates that were index-linked; then, later, index-linked gilts subject to bonus increases measured by inflation increases. Wonderful when inflation runs, so you buy on your own judgement. See also *Granny bonds*.

INDIRECT TAX   For example, Value Added Tax (VAT); often described as painless extraction because, by paying the tax indirectly (sometimes in concealed form), you don't feel the pain as you do when you see your deductions on the payslip or send off a cheque to the taxman. Many economists think all taxes should be indirect.

INDUSTRIAL AND COMMERCIAL FINANCE CORPORATION/ICFC   A subsidiary of Investors in Industry, which is owned by the Bank of England and the clearing banks. ICFC lends or channels money into young or new businesses, new industries, etc. Not given to backing starters but to putting money into going concerns.

INFLATION Is there a soul who doesn't know what this means? Rising prices, rising incomes, though not always in the parallel we should like. We have all ended up hardly recognizing the value of money as our parents and grandparents did. They talk of wages in the 1930s being £3 a week, and we laugh. But dining out cost 1s. 6d. (now 7½p) then, and a weekly rent was counted in shillings (5p pieces). One of us authors has lived through deflation and nil inflation. Quite a memory, that is.

INHERITANCE TAX Fairly new, a kind of modernized replacement of the old Estate Duty. A tax on assets at one's death, paid by the estate of the deceased before bequests in the will are distributed. Exemptions or part exemptions aim to keep together family businesses, farms, etc. No such tax on bequests to spouses.

INLAND REVENUE The big takeaway department of government, the one that calculates how much tax we are due to pay and also collects it through HM Collectors of Taxes. They do not handle V A T and Customs duty, which come under the Customs and Excise Department.

INSIDER DEALINGS Illegal share dealings by insiders acting on knowledge not available to the rest of the public who own shares in a company.

INSOLVENT Broke, unable to pay debts. Applies to people or companies — see *Bankrupt*.

INSURANCE Cover against loss, injury, death, theft and a host of other things. You pay premiums to a company which promises you agreed sums in specified circumstances. Some famous film stars of old insured their legs, bosoms (or busts, as they were then called), hair, foreign accents, voices — anything that helped them to riches or fame.

INTEREST The money paid for the right to use a capital loan from anyone. The borrower pays the interest to the lender. Some is fixed, some is variable, some just unpredictable because it may be based on profit made by the loan.

INTERNATIONAL MONETARY FUND IMF is the best-known abbreviation. Based in Washington, backed by most world countries, reporting to the United Nations. All countries contribute an agreed sum in their own currencies. Members may borrow to see them through short-term problems, usually in their *Balance of payments*. If a country over-borrows, the IMF tinkers with and demands changes in that country's government and economic policy. Longer-term lending is through the *World Bank*.

INTER VIVOS A tax term used in its Latin form, meaning during life, as of gifts.

INTESTATE   Without a will.

INSTITUTIONS   The big battalions of the money world, such as pension funds, insurance companies, unit trusts, investment trusts. Holders of most of the country's shares, powerful weapons in takeover bids. Popular with company managements because they are steady investors rather than speculators, gamblers. They tend to stand by their companies.

INVESTORS IN INDUSTRY   see *Industrial and Commercial Finance Corporation.*

ISSUED CAPITAL   The part of a company's authorized capital that has been issued by way of shares or similar sales or exchanges.

JOB   What you are after with a bank.

KEYNES   Lord Keynes, born John Maynard Keynes in 1883, died 1946. Famous economist who believed the state should 'prime the pump'. He meant that the state should stimulate public spending (by the state, of course). He helped to set up the *IMF*. His Keynesian theories are still much discussed. Hard to work in finance without hearing of Keynes (pronounced Keens or, by some, Kanes).

KRUGERRAND   South African coin containing exactly one ounce of gold. Easy way of investing in gold, though you pay for the labour of minting it as well as for the gold. Banks buy and sell them, among other dealers. In Britain you pay VAT on top of the price.

LAISSER FAIRE   Economists' language to describe a policy of letting market forces operate without government control or interference.

LEADERS AND LAGGARDS   Popular way of describing shares or companies that do well or badly. Top and bottom of that league. Thought to have been coined by the FT, which ran a regular column under that heading.

LEAK   Abhorred and loved by the City, according to whether it makes shares go up or down. Leaked knowledge (often rumour) of bids, company activity. In politics, what a politician may use to test public reaction. Before he does it, that is, whatever 'it' may be.

LEGAL TENDER   Money that must be accepted in settlement of debt. Copper may be refused if coins total more than 20p. In 1979 a boy, fined for skateboarding where he should not have done, tried to pay the fine with the copper contents of his money box, and was refused until he got his small change converted into legal tender. How officious some officials can be. 5p and 10p coins should add up to no more than £5, and £1 coins, 50p pieces and 20p pieces to no more than £10.

LIBRA, LIBRI £ or £s, from Latin. The L of l.s.d., symbols of pre-decimal money. See *Solidus, Denarius.*

LICENSED DEPOSIT TAKERS The second category of firms allowed to take deposits from the public under the Banking Act 1979. The first category includes the banks. Despite being 'second-class', deposit takers do not get licences unless they are 'competently and prudently' managed. LDTs cannot call themselves banks. Only the Bank of England can decide whether a bank really is a bank.

LIFE INSURANCE Insuring your life so that dependants get some financial compensation on your death. Several varieties. See *Insurance.*

LIFFE Pronounced life. A market near the Bank of England which deals in contracts to deliver money, foreign currency and other forms of hard finance at some future date. Started in 1982, got off to very slow start, now coming to life.

LIMITED COMPANY A legal enterprise that issues shares at a value called par value (subsequent dealings and supply/demand ratios will alter the price, not the par value). The liability of the shareholders is limited to the par value in the event of disaster. There are private or public limited companies. The former has only 'private' shareholders. The latter's shares are on sale to the public, and these are now called PLCs where once they were simply called 'Limited'. Interestingly, the 'PLC' must always be printed or written as it was first written when the changeover or application to be one occurred. There being no rule at that time, the 'PLC' is in many forms – all capital letters, all non-capitals, the first letter in capitals, the 'LC' not, having full stops between the letters or not. A company limited by guarantee, normally a charity, is one into which shareholders do not put money in advance but guarantee to pay up if the company goes bust.

LIQUID The state of having readily convertible assets, like money or bonds or stocks, that can rapidly become hard cash. Government stocks are very liquid, antiques and jewellery less so.

LIQUIDATOR The man who is appointed by creditors to wind up a business, meet the debts and share out the residue among shareholders. Normally a specialist accountant. See *Receiver.*

LLOYD'S OF LONDON Actually the Corporation of Lloyd's. Works along the lines of the Stock Exchange but deals in insurance, catering mainly for large commercial insurance, though also dealing in life, cars and such. There have been a few problems in recent years, and Lloyd's is aiming to set its house in better order while under scrutiny.

LOAN   We all know what that is.

LOAN GUARANTEE SCHEME   The government guarantees loans for small companies to encourage banks to lend.

LONDON COMMODITY EXCHANGE   Like the Stock Exchange but dealing in commodities rather than money – wool, coffee, grain, sugar, cocoa, etc.

LONDON ENTERPRISE AGENCY   Tries to help small businesses with advice and contacts, training and introducing lenders or investors. Set up by, among others, Barclays Bank, Midland Bank, Shell, BP, Marks & Spencer, *ICFC*, IBM, GEC, etc.

LONDON METAL EXCHANGE   As the name implies, a kind of Stock Exchange dealing in metals but not in gold.

LONG   Either a *gilt* due for redemption in 10–15 years or a Stock Exchange jargon word. If you go long on a share you have bought a lot of them. You have been a *bull*.

MATCHING   The final check at the end of the day that buyer and seller agree on the deal, the number bought or sold and the prices. Applies to financial and commodity markets.

MINI-BUDGET   A phrase of the last 15 or so years. Chancellors have from time to time made financial or fiscal proposals between the main springtime Budgets – Denis Healey was a prime mini-budgeteer. The interim budgets are mini-budgets.

MIRAS   Mortgage Investment Relief at Source. Relief meaning tax relief on mortgage payments (on part, not all). Terror strikes all as rumours surface from time to time that such relief will one day be stopped, as was tax relief on insurance premiums.

MONEY MARKET   In the City, it deals with short-term loans between banks, companies, local authorities, etc.

MONEY SUPPLY   Basically bank deposits, notes and coins in circulation, as it were. Economists and the Treasury use numbered codes to pinpoint which money supply they mean. M1 is chiefly notes, coins, bank deposits. M3 is M1 plus deposits with foreign banks in Britain, merchant banks, discount houses and the like.

MONOPOLIES AND MERGERS COMMISSION   A government agency which investigates, on behalf of the Secretary of State for Trade, mergers, monopolies and practices that are not in the public interest or threaten not to be. Can prevent over-monopolistic things happening (for example a major merger), but cannot break down existing monopolies as they can in America, where companies can be ordered to divest themselves of some operations.

MONOPOLY   If there is only one seller, maker, provider of a product or service, that's a monopoly, giving the provider power to control prices and supplies. In fact the buyers decide how much control, since they can refuse to buy. Nationalized industries like gas and electricity are monopolies, though they deny it, claiming they compete with each other. Two firms or people hogging a market create a duopoly.

MONOPSONY   A buyer's monopoly. There is only one buyer for any product or service.

MORTGAGE   The loan that enables people to buy their homes. Offered by banks, building societies and, on rare occasions, private individuals or consortia. Various kinds, for example endowment mortgage, option mortgage, etc.

MUTUAL FUND   As near as dammit American unit trust, though there are differences.

NAKED WRITER   An idiot, foolhardy investor who 'writes', or sells, shares he does not own. He gambles that the price of the shares will fall before he has to deliver them, so that he can buy them for delivery at less than his selling price. Profitable if he's right, but he loses more than his shirt if wrong. Hence naked.

NATIONAL CONSUMER COUNCIL   Government-sponsored body which investigates and reports on laws, operations illegal or legal, circumstances that affect customers, highlighting goodies and baddies alike. Published a report on the banks in December 1983 (see Chapter 6).

NATIONAL ECONOMIC DEVELOPMENT COUNCIL   Neddy is its popular name. Aims to 'co-ordinate all the major expansion plans of British industry'. Started in 1962; staff are led by the Chancellor of the Exchequer; includes representatives of industry and trade unions. A lot of 'little Neddies' exist, each specializing in its own industry.

NATIONAL INSURANCE   An innovation of Lloyd George in 1911. Based on insurance practice: each of us pays a premium on our earnings to fund unemployment and sickness or disability benefits, old age pensions (now called the State Retirement Pension) and other largesses of the state to its people.

NATIONALIZED INDUSTRIES   Industries owned by you and me, the taxpayers. A socialist concept that does more or less work for railways, electricity and such, but one that the Conservative Party believes wrong on the basis that competition generates better value for consumers of the goods or services, hence privatization.

NATIONAL SAVINGS   The government body that banks, as it were, through Post Offices. The department runs investment accounts, savings certificates, premium bonds, save-as-you-earn schemes, index-linked schemes, ordinary accounts and so forth.

NET   What is left after deductions, debts, taxes and such. The net profit is what the company has left. Your net income is what's left for you. See *Gross.*

NET ASSET VALUE   The shareholders' funds, minus invisibles like goodwill, are divided by the number of issued shares to get the NAV per share. If the NAV is greater than the share price you are on terra firma, but perhaps the management could be putting the assets to work harder for the company good. If the NAV is less than the share price, the company is popular but could be at risk if disasters strike.

NO-CLAIMS BONUS   What you get for not making claims on your motor insurance. You get no cash, just a discount on your premiums up to as much as 60 per cent. Makes some claims not worth pursuing, which is what insurers hope will happen.

NUMBERED BANK ACCOUNT   Though traditionally Swiss, offered by many countries. The account is identified only by a number, known solely to the bank and the account-holder. Theoretically secret even from tax or criminal investigators, though that secrecy is giving way a little to suspected major criminal investigations.

OFFICE OF FAIR TRADING/OFT   The Department of Trade's watchdog. Looks at mergers above £15m and decides whether or not to refer them for investigation by the *Monopolies and Mergers Commission.* Also investigates various trades, publicizes results to heighten public awareness or to promote statutory changes.

OLD LADY   See *Bank of England*, nicknamed the Old Lady of Threadneedle Street.

OLIGOPOLY   A market dominated by a few sellers. See *Monopoly*.

ORDINARY DIVIDEND   The dividend on ordinary shares.

OVERDRAFT   Don't just run one or there may be cash penalties and, in any case, it gets you a bad reputation at the bank and will affect you when you do want one. If you need one, ask for it and arrange it properly. You may need a banker's reference one day, and his assessment depends much on how you run your bank account. Overdrafts may be cheaper ways of borrowing than personal loans, which banks tend to prefer.

OVER THE COUNTER MARKET   An unofficial stock market with a small but increasing number of operators – perhaps you saw them advertising for people to sell their British Telecom and British Gas shares through them. They also buy and sell shares in a sort of personal list of companies which may not yet be floated or quoted but want a feel of who their shareholders are and what they expect.

OVERHEADS   The fixed costs that you cannot avoid, the ones that are with you whether you trade or not. The building, salaries, the heat, the light, that kind of thing.

PAR VALUE   See *Nominal value*. Not often the same as market value on shares, bonds, etc.

PAY AS YOU EARN   The tax you pay on earned income, deducted as you earn it before you get the change. Usually known simply by its letters as PAYE.

PAYOLA   A bribe, a pay-off, a bonus. Usually signifies something underhand, unethical.

PENNY   The old penny is the coin of which you used to have 240 to the pound. The new penny is 100 to the pound. See *Denarius*.

PERSONAL ALLOWANCE   The tax free slab of income, changing from Budget to Budget, allowed before tax is due. Single person's, married, age, disability and various allowances are defined by the Inland Revenue. Some are automatically granted, others need to be claimed, though they are a right. The Inland Revenue doesn't know if you are above age and on limited income, disabled or whatever. You need to tell them.

PETTY CASH   The small sums for which few firms expect detailed accounts. Office tea, extra paper clips, that kind of thing. Most purchases are made in bulk and carefully accounted for, but some kind of financial float exists in many offices and organizations. Small firms that do not buy bulk purchases often have bigger petty cash floats.

PINK FORM   The form that gives you preferential treatment when applying for new shares. Often pink. Sent to existing shareholders or to employees of companies when new shares are on offer.

PLACING   The private selling of a block of shares in a public quoted company, Not liked by the Stock Exchange, especially if sold for less than current market price, but sometimes the result of a takeover bid where the shares cannot normally be sold on the open market.

PLOUGHING BACK   The ploughing back of profits into such amenities as new premises, new business, anything instead of giving dividends to shareholders.

PLOUGHSHARES   In the non-biblical sense, shares that are given to shareholders instead of dividend. Hated and rare, but could be useful to businesses temporarily short of cash.

PORTFOLIO   A company's or person's collection of investments, mainly in stocks and shares, though there are property portfolios and other portfolios.

PREFERENCE SHARES   These have priority over ordinary shares for dividends and repayment in the event of a break-up. May or may not have more voting power.

PREMIUM   Either the sum above the par or floated value of a share; or the sum you pay to insurance companies for the cover or benefits they promise.

PREMIUM BOND   The national lottery. No interest, but your bond goes into the draw for prizes from £50 to £250,000. See Ernie.

PRICE EARNINGS RATIO/PE   A company's share price divided by the earnings per share.

PRIVATIZE   New word for 'denationalize'. What the Conservatives do to nationalized industries.

PROBATE   The certificate of proving a will, meaning that the executor can start disposing of the property of a dead person's estate.

PROFESSION What banking is. And being an actor, solicitor, doctor, accountant, or priest. Now embraces many former 'trades'. Used to be much distinction between the two. Gradually dying. Professionalism means good at the job.

PROFIT What you make over and above the total cost of what you sell. In business, the difference between annual costs and annual turnover. Can be net or gross. The price you paid must include all costs – the raw material, the loss of interest on the cash that bought it, the storage, the labour to give it added value, anything. People and companies who forget that watch their apparent profits disappear.

PUBLIC LIMITED COMPANIES See *Limited company*. A PLC must have 2 or more members; a nominal share capital of £50,000 or more, of which at least 25 per cent must be fully paid up; and a memorandum and articles of association outlining its own rules. PLCs can offer their shares to the public.

PUBLIC SECTOR Central and local government, nationalized industries, Bank of England, hence the following item.

PUBLIC SECTOR BORROWING REQUIREMENT/PSBR The Chancellor's term for accounting the difference between the public sector's income and its spending. Need not actually entail borrowing.

QUOTED A company that sells its shares is a quoted company, meaning quoted on the Stock Exchange or the Unlisted Securities Market (USM). The *Financial Times* prints the quotes, or prices, of the shares. To get a quote, to be public, to float.

RAT RACE What you are less likely to be in if you go into banking. Accurately, the blind pursuit of success, rushing headlong like rats rushed behind the Pied Piper. Has become known as the stressful competitive business of being in business. Everyone thinks they long to escape, most want to join.

RECEIVER The accountant or other person appointed by creditors to liquidate a company's assets and settle whatever may be available to creditors. See *Liquidator*.

RECESSION A kind of euphemism for a depression or slump. Gives the impression of temporary economic downturns. See *Boom*, *Slump*, *Depression*.

REDEMPTION Of gilts and insurance bonds, etc. The final repayment, as agreed, and the time agreed, the redemption date.

REDUNDANCY PAYMENT   Golden or leaden headshake, compensation for loss of job if, indeed, anything can compensate. The government runs a fund built up from employers' contributions under the Social Security Act. Companies can draw from it if forced either to go into liquidation or to make redundancies in order to preserve the remaining jobs, to keep afloat.

REFLATION   The act or period of improving the economy, of getting inflation going after a spell of deflation or static economy. Manipulated by government or just by sheer good luck, but rare in recent times. Not needed.

REINSURANCE   Insurance companies hedge their bets by laying off big deals, reinsuring so that part of the risk is carried by others.

RESERVES   Sums of money kept back out of profits to meet sudden, often unpredictable, expenditure. Governments have gold reserves. Companies have cash or similar kinds.

RETAIL BANKING   Jargon for branch banking, anything directly connected with personal customers.

RIGHTS ISSUE   Shares issued by a company wanting to raise more money without actually borrowing it. New shares are created but must be approved at shareholders' meetings held after due notice. Usually sold at a discount on the current share price to attract buyers. Existing shareholders get priority rights and may sell their rights. Tend to hang fire in bad times; at any rate, tend temporarily to depress the share price.

ROYALTY   A fee for work, a percentage due on recent sales of such work. Usually applies to authors, artists and others who 'sell' their copyrights in return for a fee on unit sales, but also applies in business where licences, know-how, patents and other such things are sold between companies. Almost always a percentage, though there are agreed cash royalties.

SALARY   Agreed weekly pay, different from wages not only in the snobbish sense but because it is paid no matter what hours or work output may be (though employers would not remain silent if you didn't give what you are paid for). *Wages* are paid according to work done. 'Salary' derives from Roman money given to soldiers to buy salt.

SAVE AS YOU EARN   A kind of savings contract. Saving by instalments. Operated by government and building societies.

SCRIP   A share issue, a *capitalization issue*. Allegedly free shares, but they are not.

SECOND MORTGAGE   The downfall of many, because punishing rates of interest are often charged for these. You have a mortgage of £25,000 on a house worth £50,000. You can borrow a percentage of the difference on a second mortgage, and the second company has only second call on your money if and when the house is sold. Hence the higher rate for the higher risk. Normally done by finance houses, though most building societies and banks will extend existing mortgages more cheaply.

SHARES   A company's authorized capital is split into shares, of which, even for private companies, there must be at least two. The shares are sold; shareholders can own small or large slices of 'their' companies and have voting and other rights, including a right to share in the profits (or losses) by means of dividends. Publicly quoted companies' shares are traded on the Stock Exchange.

SHELL   Jargon for a company which, though more or less bereft of assets and possibly not even trading, still has a quote on the Stock Exchange. Appeals to those wanting to get in by the back door and avoid the cost and hassle of floating. The newcomer injects his assets and forges ahead with an automatic quote.

SHILLING   The old pre-decimalization coin, of which there were 20 to the £1. Oddly, the middle letter of l.s.d. the old monetary symbol did not stand for shilling but for solidus, used mostly in the plural, solidi, from the Latin.

SHORT   Going short of a stock or a share means going a bear; promising to deliver stock you haven't got, hoping to buy back later at a lower price. See *Naked writer*.

SLUMP   What it sounds like but in money terms. See *Recession*, *Depression*, *Boom*.

SOCIAL SECURITY   The government system that aims to alleviate financial hardship, to see that nobody starves or is ill without medical treatment, is cold or homeless, that children do not go in need. Some four-fifths of the cost comes from National Insurance contributions, made by those of us who can afford them or are earning, the rest from benevolent government. In theory, we have all contributed and we get back something on a kind of insurance system. In fact, some never can or do contribute but still get help.

SOFT CURRENCY   See *Hard currency*.

SOLIDUS, SOLIDI   See *Shilling*.

SPECULATOR   A gambler with investments.

SQUARE MILE   See *City of London*. The original London, always and still the core of the money business.

SQUEEZE   Pressure on the economy to squeeze out overspending and, hopefully, inflationary demand. Once often put on by government, but less so in the last 15 years. Also applies to money-men pushing up prices to squeeze out the bears, who have sold high hoping to see prices lower before they have to buy and deliver. Thus a bear squeeze.

STAG   Another Stock Exchange animal. One who applies for new shares, or shares in companies which come to the market for the first time free of most expenses. If in great demand and oversubscribed the shares go to a premium, making a profit for the stag, who never intended to keep them and bought them only to resell. Thousands of stags sold their British Telecom shares at double the price in the first week. Stags can be caught with their antlers down if a new share proves unpopular, in poor demand. The price goes to a discount and they have to sell at a loss.

STAMP DUTY   A tax on the transfer of property or, sometimes, money. By law a stamp must be bought to stick on the documents. Comes under Inland Revenue. The buyer pays, unless there is a private agreement to the contrary.

STALE CHEQUE   More than 6 months old, no good.

STANDING ORDER   An order to your bank to pay out the same sum on the same date at fixed intervals – often monthly but can be quarterly, half yearly or annually. The bank charges you for doing it. See *Direct debit*.

STOCKBROKER   Deals in stocks and shares on the Stock Exchange. See *Broker*.

STOCK EXCHANGE   The market for selling and buying stocks, shares and similar securities, as they are normally called. Exists in most countries, London's 'International Stock Exchange' being one of the three biggest together with New York and Tokyo. London is actually part of a bunch of UK exchanges, because they exist in many of the major provincial cities though they sometimes have London offices. The name also refers to the building in which the market operates, a skyscraper hard by the Bank of England with offices for staff, stockbrokers, etc. Trading was done on 'the Floor'. However, dealing is now handled electronically between brokers and 'the Floor' is closed. The Stock Exchange does still provide the marketplace, but it does so now through its computers. The motto is 'My word is my bond', and deals are done on trust until confirmed by contract notes. A constantly updated list gives all quoted securities, their dividends, and all prices at which *bargains* have been marked. Also listed are the unlisted securities, believe it or not.

STOP-GO   Brake-and-accelerator economics of many post-war governments trying to keep up with natural market forces or to manipulate them. The Thatcher government has done its best to avoid such changeable policies and to stick to a consistent line, so much so that the phrase is dying.

STOP-LOSS   A standing instruction from investors to banks or stockbrokers to buy or sell within a pre-specified price band. Stops buying at wilder prices if prices rise or fall very steeply.

SUBSIDIARY   A company controlled by another company.

TAKEOVER   When one company acquires another, usually by making a bid for the shares direct to the shareholders. All get the same offer, all get the chance to read attacking, defending, counter-attacking documents about the pros and cons of A acquiring B. The shareholder decides and holds or sells his shares. A takeover does not go ahead until at least half the shares are sold to the bidder. Once the bidder has 90 per cent he is legally entitled to take over the balance.

TAX   When you are earning, you'll know all about this. What the government takes from your income. See *Avoidance*, *Evasion*.

TAX CODE   Your allowances are worked out and the Inland Revenue gives you a Code which is the basis for your PAYE deductions. You get notice of your Code and can appeal if it seems wrong.

TAX HAVEN   A place in which to live and pay less tax than in Britain, for example, the Channel Islands, the Isle of Man, little pockets in the West Indies or in Europe, etc. They may seem attractive, but they may have an expensive cost of living to offset tax advantages. Also, do you want to be a tax exile, friendless, rootless, far from family?

TRAVELLERS' CHEQUES   Paper money negotiable almost anywhere in the world; useless until signed by the owner as he gets the cash, thus pretty safe. All the banks issue them or get them for you, and they can be in any major currency. If lost, stolen or strayed, they will be automatically repaid but it takes time.

TREASURY   The government department responsible for the nation's financial and economic policy, supervising spending, taxes, borrowing, development and overseas or foreign exchange rates vis-à-vis our own.

TREASURY BILLS   Paper money in denominations of £5,000, £10,000 or £50,000. They entitle the holder to payment of such sums in 91 days (sometimes different timing). The means by which government borrows for short periods. Bills do not necessarily sell at par value but to the highest bidder.

TREATY OF ROME   The Treaty under which the Common Market operates, its own rules. Somewhat debased in its nearly 30 years of life.

TRILLION   Used to be a million times a million million, but we have adopted the American trillion which is simply a million times a million. See *Billion*.

TRUST, TRUSTEE   A legal agreement for trustees to manage assets for others. Young children might have money left to them in trust until they reach a certain age or comply with certain conditions. Trustees may or may not be related, but normally include at least one professional firm or representative. Banks do a good deal of trustee business.

TURNOVER   A company's income or earnings.

UNDERWRITER   One who writes his name under a legal document to guarantee it. He will pay in the event of default or if the price is not forthcoming for other reasons. A share issue can be underwritten. Brokers, bankers or a consortium guarantee the capital. They will then own the shares the public has not wanted to buy and these might later rise. Meanwhile the company has the use of all the money it hoped to raise. Also an insurance term.

UNLISTED SECURITIES MARKET   Part of the Stock Exchange, started in 1980 so that small companies could get a share quote and so sell their shares to the public without the high cost of a full quotation. Though USM shares are said to be risky, and certainly they reveal less information than fully-quoted shares, many have performed really glamorously. See *Over the counter*.

VALUE ADDED TAX/VAT   Indirect taxation. Customs and Excise collects it. A percentage decreed by government is imposed on goods from the manufacturing stage, and added at each new production stage, until you and I buy it and we just have nobody to pass it down to, do we? Input tax and output tax are checked against each other and some companies get refunds, others are always paying because of the special equipment they need. Some goods are exempt, like food, Some are zero-rated, like gas and electricity, which means a tax can be slapped on both or either without further warning – government simply raises the rate from zero to whatever it decides. Not, one hopes, to the full extent of 15 per cent. Indeed, hopefully not at all.

VENTURE CAPITAL   Capital for new and struggling firms. Finance houses, sometimes banks and others provide it, usually to the extent of more than 50 per cent because that gives them the right and the chance to keep a close eye on things. Mostly provided by specialist finance houses who understand mad inventors, crazy idealists, clever technologists and others who usually know little or nothing about money, never have any, but will work round the clock on what they think is a winning idea.

WAGES   Pay for work done, normally on a piece-work (by the unit) basis. Often means pay by the hour.

WASTING ASSETS   Any asset which is going to need replacing in the foreseeable future because it is wearing out, falling down, becoming unproductive or out of date. A lease with a declining span, old machinery, etc.

WHOLESALE BANKING   Large-scale banking; big finance with other banks, companies, local authorities, etc. Cost-efficient from a bank's viewpoint. See *Retail banking.*

WORKING CAPITAL   Money needed and used for the daily running of the business, to pay the wages, the heat, the light and similar outlays.

WORLD BANK   The Robin Hood of the world? Well, maybe just a little bit. Originally set up to help countries recover from the Second World War, taking from the rich to lend to the poor – loans normally lasting up to 20 years. Cheapest loans for poor countries are for development, through a special division. There was a formal name, the International Bank for Reconstruction and Development.

VIABILITY   The ability to pay one's way and hopefully to make profits; the state of being able to pay one's debts.

ZERO GROWTH   The ultimate undesirable, the economist's phrase for no economic progress.

Z-SCORE   A method of checking a company's health, especially if it seems like going broke. Balance sheets of many years are studied for cash flow, current ratio, debt-equity ratio and such. The experts then jigsaw the conclusions, with which they are inordinately cautious, not wishing to precipitate a rush on the company by creditors who could cause the final shut-down.

FOR THE BEST IN PAPERBACKS, LOOK FOR THE

In every corner of the world, on every subject under the sun, Penguin represents quality and variety – the very best in publishing today.

For complete information about books available from Penguin – including Pelicans, Puffins, Peregrines and Penguin Classics – and how to order them, write to us at the appropriate address below. Please note that for copyright reasons the selection of books varies from country to country.

In the United Kingdom: For a complete list of books available from Penguin in the U.K., please write to *Dept E.P., Penguin Books Ltd, Harmondsworth, Middlesex, UB7 0DA*

In the United States: For a complete list of books available from Penguin in the U.S., please write to *Dept BA, Penguin, 299 Murray Hill Parkway, East Rutherford, New Jersey 07073*

In Canada: For a complete list of books available from Penguin in Canada, please write to *Penguin Books Canada Ltd, 2801 John Street, Markham, Ontario L3R 1B4*

In Australia: For a complete list of books available from Penguin in Australia, please write to the *Marketing Department, Penguin Books Australia Ltd, P.O. Box 257, Ringwood, Victoria 3134*

In New Zealand: For a complete list of books available from Penguin in New Zealand, please write to the *Marketing Department, Penguin Books (NZ) Ltd, Private Bag, Takapuna, Auckland 9*

In India: For a complete list of books available from Penguin, please write to *Penguin Overseas Ltd, 706 Eros Apartments, 56 Nehru Place, New Delhi, 110019*

In Holland: For a complete list of books available from Penguin in Holland, please write to *Penguin Books Nederland B.V., Postbus 195, NL–1380AD Weesp, Netherlands*

In Germany: For a complete list of books available from Penguin, please write to *Penguin Books Ltd, Friedrichstrasse 10 – 12, D–6000 Frankfurt Main 1, Federal Republic of Germany*

In Spain: For a complete list of books available from Penguin in Spain, please write to *Longman Penguin España, Calle San Nicolas 15, E–28013 Madrid, Spain*

FOR THE BEST IN PAPERBACKS, LOOK FOR THE 🐧

PENGUIN DICTIONARIES

Archaeology

Architecture

Art and Artists

Biology

Botany

Building

Chemistry

Civil Engineering

Commerce

Computers

Decorative Arts

Design and Designers

Economics

English and European
  History

English Idioms

Geography

Geology

Historical Slang

Literary Terms

Mathematics

Microprocessors

Modern History 1789–1945

Modern Quotations

Physical Geography

Physics

Political Quotations

Politics

Proverbs

Psychology

Quotations

Religions

Saints

Science

Sociology

Surnames

Telecommunications

The Theatre

Troublesome Words

Twentieth Century History

FOR THE BEST IN PAPERBACKS, LOOK FOR THE 🐧

PENGUIN BUSINESS

Great management classics of the world (with brand new Introductions by leading contemporary figures); widely studied business textbooks; and exciting new business titles covering all the major areas of interest for today's businessman and businesswoman.

Parkinson's Law or **The Pursuit of Progress** C. Northcote Parkinson
My Years with General Motors Alfred P. Sloan Jr
Self-Help Samuel Smiles
The Spirit of Enterprise George Gilder
Dinosaur & Co: Studies in Corporate Evolution Tom Lloyd
Understanding Organizations Charles B. Handy
The Art of Japanese Management Richard Tanner Pascale & Anthony G. Athos
Modern Management Methods Ernest Dale & L. C. Michelon
Lateral Thinking for Management Edward de Bono
The Winning Streak Workout Book Walter Goldsmith & David Clutterbuck
The Social Psychology of Industry J. A. C. Brown
Offensive Marketing J. H. Davidson
The Anatomy of Decisions Peter G. Moore & H. Thomas
The Human Side of Enterprise Douglas McGregor
Corporate Recovery Stuart Slatter